Where the Wild Poppies Grow

Kevin Bell

Published by New Generation Publishing in 2019

Copyright © Kevin Bell 2019

First Edition

The author asserts the moral right under the Copyright, Designs and Patents Act 1988 to be identified as the author of this work.

All Rights reserved. No part of this publication may be reproduced, stored in a retrieval system or transmitted, in any form or by any means without the prior consent of the author, nor be otherwise circulated in any form of binding or cover other than that which it is published and without a similar condition being imposed on the subsequent purchaser.

ISBN 978-1-78955-681-0

www.newgeneration-publishing.com

New Generation Publishing

"Faces of The Fallen"

In memory of every British Soldier killed in Afghanistan. Painted by Arabella Dorman for Westminster Abbey's Field of Remembrance, November 2012 ©

Contents

Come walk with me 5
A Bosnian Moment 6
Epitaph 7
The Warrior 9
George 10
Heal The Flag 13
Repatriation 15
RAF Lyneham 17
Boy Soldiers 18
Coldstream Guards 20
London 23
Earth 25
Annual Appraisal 26
Poet 27
Companions 28
Burnham Abbey 29
The Dubliner 30
Blue Collar 32
De Mob 35
Parade 37
Sandhurst Chapel 40
Woolwich 42
Armistice 44
Clueless 46
Island Race 48
Rank 51
Remember 53
The Reunion 56
Homecoming 58
Embers 60

Flanders' Memorial Garden 62
I am what I am 64
Where Watchmen wait 66
The Veteran's wife 67
Sky Taxi 69
Great War days 71
Where soldiers dream! 74
Where none can see 75
Chief Joseph 78
The Last Bugle 79
Where heroes passed 81
Something New 83
Through the eye of the storm 84
Song Writing 86
Notes.. 88
About the Author 111
From the Author 113
Published Papers 115
The Heart and the Heat of Battle 116
Remembrance Sunday 128
The British Soldier... 141
About the Artist 157

List of illustrations

Faces of the Fallen	Front Cover
A Long Way From Home	8
Through a Glass	13
A Good Shoulder	18
"Sleepless"	22
Al Basrah	24
The Dubliner	30
Wazha Pa Wazha (Shoulder to Shoulder), Afghanistan	32
Another Beautiful Day in Shaibah, Iraq	46
A Moment's Respite	48
On Patrol	53
Waiting in a Warrior	57
Taqalla Baraye, Zenda Mandan (The Struggle to Survive)	60
The Medical Emergency Response Team (MERT)	69
Dawn over the Sheet al-Arab	73
Safe Return	81
The Dance	83
Above the City	87
On Patrol	117
A Quick Turn Around	129
Downtown, Basra	142

A Mirror For The 20th Century	150
Back to Base	151
Holding On	152
I Am Strong	153
The Return, Sangin, Afghanistan	154

Foreword

"The salvation of this human world lies nowhere else than in the human heart, in the human power to reflect, in human meekness and human responsibility. It takes an artist to see the world in this way."
Vaclav Havel.

"How true it is that big things can hang on little words."
Padre Kevin.

It is a great honour to have been asked to write a foreword to what is not simply a collection of poems, but a great canvas, on which a whole life has been drawn. Padre Kevin paints a portrait of the British Solider, but he also draws a self portrait and in doing so, reveals himself as a man of profound integrity, *"excavating"* as he says, *"through the layers"* of his life.

To read these poems is to be taken on an urgent journey through those layers. Grounded in present struggle, Padre Kevin's words go back to past remembrances that are the bedrock of his life, whilst simultaneously allowing the reader to move forward to the possibility of hope, redemption and the great mystery of love, that lies at the heart of faith.

Etched with courage and remarkable honesty, these poems are an expose of the human soul, and what it means to be alive in today's world; to struggle, to wrestle, to doubt and to heal. They are an attempt to make something of experience, and the faces and places, successes and failures of a life, through the intimate language of poetry. These are personal confessions that relate to a bigger whole, as Padre Kevin writes, *"I am just a funnel, filter or prism for all those people, years and experiences."*

In doing so, he reminds each of us of our own individual responsibility: and the importance of maintaining an ethical core, within the grim realities of modern day warfare. His words reach for the universal within the particular.

This is a collection of work where the light meets the darkness. Where love and faith can begin to heal the broken, the wounded, the bereaved. To read it is a lesson in morality and the selfless desire to reach out to our fellow human beings, and to all those who struggle, doubt, love and have lost.

Throughout his poetry, Padre Kevin trades on the aesthetics of compassion rather than politics, revealing the weight of responsibility that he has carried throughout his career, from the Balkans to Afghanistan, as well as his profound sense of honour in serving,

"I have remembered these all once were children"

His words, like the subject of these poems dance on the surface, yet speak of hidden depths. They are a call to pay attention to the preciousness of life and the beat of each individual, struggling soul.

They bring before us the triumph and sorrow of soldiering – the courage, dignity, humility and commitment to be a force for good in this troubled world. These are poems that will not let us forget the ultimate sacrifice paid by so many. They are a tribute to the bereaved and the wounded, and a recognition of the love of families and comrades who stitch together what war had torn apart.

The ruins of a young man's life
A broken throne for every wife

The Padre speaks as a parent, as a son, as a husband, as a brother, as a comrade. He writes for the families who have lost their son, for the solider who can never express what he has endured. He writes as his own confession, drawing on *"deeper things"* in order to deal with the wounds that cannot be seen, the depths of human depravity unspoken. In doing so, he visualizes the invisible, and gives the voiceless a voice,

I doubt your dearest can ever know
All you had to undergo

Like the unheard soldier's stories, the Padre builds hidden depths within these poems.

This world destroys with little trace
Tattered strands of handmade lace

As the silence held on Remembrance Sunday, he hints at that which cannot be written, words that cannot be spoken, heard only in the stillness around the poems: a depth of stillness that resonates long after those poems have been read.

As an army chaplain, Padre Kevin writes in the hope that we will better understand what we ask of our armed forces and their loved ones. When the parade is over and the dignitaries have gone home, it is the military and veterans' communities that live with the consequences of what they were asked to do.

These are poems about their sacrifice, about loss, remembrance, comradeship, good fighting and the extraordinary courage and professionalism of the British Soldier. They offer us fragments of a broken world, with unflinching honesty and a courage that is born out of faith, the courage to confess doubt and to renew through love. To read them is to heal, to wash the wounds with hope and knowledge of eternal life.

In writing this collection of works, Padre Kevin shows us that God is not in the event, but in the response, and reveals that we are all free to make the choice between revenge and hatred or forgiveness & love. These are poems born out of the darkness yet they are full of the possibility of light. To quote the great thirteenth century mystic, Rumi *"the wound is the place where the light enters you"*.

I urge you to read these poems slowly, they are an expression of deep wounds, but wounds that are full of light.

Arabella Dorman
War Artist and Portrait painter
London

Come walk with me [1]

I have safely walked passed fields of corn
Where the wild poppies grow
There to pause a while and dip my eyes
In those many pools of blood
For they bandage tight with silence
A secret we ought to know
It is the legend that flowers like these
Will only rise
Where some soldier fell
With a thud…

I have pondered deep the carefree wind
Which plays about their form
And wallowed in my children's laughter
Borne so light within its arms
Such happiness, such promise
Such memories now the norm
Yet beneath these feet lie rich young lives
Who died to make this so
At peace though much forgotten
In the soil of family farms…

I have said my "sorry" and my "thank you"
To them for all mankind
But knowing little of whom they treasured
I can only bless my own
By keeping safe these precious things
With the memorials in my mind
That when my babes as adults speak
These doves may not have flown…

I have imagined the days of other men
Perhaps dear friends have you
But dare we consider what others might think
When our days are finally threw
And will they know what we've come to know
Or safely walk passed fields of corn
Where the wild poppies
Grow…

---

[1] Written whilst serving with The Queen's Royal Lancers: Osnabruck 1996

A Bosnian Moment [2]

The wind that blows upon my face
Comes all the way from Ireland
Whilst the sun that shines upon this place
Holds precious thoughts of my land
So
Everywhere is home and every heartbeat
Free
And every faltering prayer is heard
Every sip of wine complete
That no matter where I roam
Throughout this suffering world
Nor what my eyes must see
The chalice of our Celtic Church
Is full, to the likes of me:
Breath deep, think hard
Fight well; pray true
Love much, though friends are few
For now is the time for such things
Until the Lord of all things
Is come
So
Hold fast, stand-to
Let none of the foe break through
But keep their way
Forever barred
Until this icy darkness
Melts with the rising sun
And our share in his victory
Is won

---

[2] Whilst serving with 4 Regiment Royal Artillery: Bosnia 1997

Epitaph [3]

Each man carves his own memorial
Throughout life's great tutorial
With those tools he daily finds
As each man's heart inclines

Each exhales his yesterday
For one more breathe to say and pray
Gone cares and woes like fallen foes
Yet a sore heart shows what eternity knows

Each holds tight the child in fright
At heat of day or dead of night
Releasing that love which heats the sun
Together, one more victory won

---

[3] With the 'Desert Rats' as Brigade Senior Chaplain: Kosovo 2001.

A Long Way From Home, Afghanistan

The Warrior [4]

The wounded warrior carries his pains
Through every battle for higher gains
His braking heart his troubled brow
Tell him when the time is "now"

The gentle warrior conceals his face
Through deadly arts he holds his place
With swift reply to the brutal eye
His tutored strengths help weak men try

The healing warrior by hand and sword
Brings home the hushed enduring word
His deepest peace a heavy shield
In stillness and silence his strength to wield

---

[4] With 43 Wessex Brigade as Deputy Assistant Chaplain General: Bulford Camp 2006

George [5]

(1) If St George wandered up The Mall
Anonymous as your closest Pal
Mingling hushed through Parliament Square
To see those tourists stand and stare
Would he push on along The Strand
To find old London lost and grand
Or warm his face with a winter scarf
Whilst strolling past the Cenotaph
Then marching off with memories stirred
His mantle cloaks from things absurd
The cross upon his shoulder red
For courage against all things of dread
He shields his life and cups his soul
Whilst Cabs and buses ceaseless roll
That well-worn sword hangs at his side
Here no false knight who needs to hide
With axe and lance he takes his chance
To shift the balance in life's dance
In every way his actions say
Its time my friends to "seize the day".

(2) His prayers link every chain-mail wheel
Protecting wounds that time won't heal
Faith within and strength without
Clench hidden things that give true clout
Past sellers of the next 'Big Issue'
In window panes his ghostly tissue
Veterans both in shabby clothes
Both can see a man who knows
Through chilling air forgiving sun
Restores the cost of battles won
Far from scorching Palestine
Where once he tasted bread and wine
And all the world, seemed Love to him
Though war had robbed his boyish grin
He hears that Banner flutter still
The cries of men he had to kill

---

[5] Written after a visit to London. By now I was serving with the 5th Division in Shropshire: Shawbury 2008

Now dragons of a different kind
Burn and chase his troubled mind
Dizzy with Christ who so astounds
In silence sneaks through City sounds
They spin this world the wrong way round
But every step finds holy ground
Remorse mistakes a heart that breaks
These gifts and risks a warrior takes.

(3) Level now with `Courts of Justice`
Witness here dear Truth's accomplice
Yet none have sought his testimony
Defender of all that ought to be
From pubs and shops and restaurants
He flees the modern dilettantes
Alone past `Legal Outfitters`
He seeks the ones who were no quitters
Down the narrow alley way
For the meaning of each day
Then left through so much history
He hopes to meet a mystery
Into the open court yard
Subjects worthy of The Bard
Yet every door is closed to him
Sweet choir sings out from deep within
Yes Temple Church is deaf:
To this weary pilgrim's plea
Bless dear Lord this soldier-monk:
Come home across the sea
His kindred spirits rest all twelve
Their story gives a purpose:
He cannot bear to shelve
To see them ridding upon that pillar
Is enough to make this grown man quiver
They seem so small and out of mind
These gentle knights of tender kind
They guard and spare the treasure:
Of all these islands are
Bringing home the very best:
Of cultures from afar
They pocket not the smallest bauble
They never ever dawdle
In all weathers adding value

As a cue to me and you
Cherish too our Christian ethos
And never cause it loss
Do not add to these shared riches
Before you`ve learned what all this teaches
Do not fix what is not broken
But ponder now this gallant token
Please pray for every Templar Knight
Enlist with them in life`s good fight
Remember too our friend St George
Who waits for you where dragons gorge!

Through a Glass Darkly, Afghanistan

Heal The Flag [6]

I have been a Soldier; I have been a Son
I have been your only one
I'm home from danger; become a stranger
Still darling: I'm your only one
I wore your flag upon my arm
To keep the yearning free from harm

---

[6] My second year with the 5th Division as Assistant Chaplain-General: Shawbury 2008

That they might know our liberty
I wore your flag upon my arm

I've been a Lover; I've been a friend
I was faithful to the end
With my comrades; I laughed and cried
We were faithful to the end
We wore your flag upon our arm
To keep the yearning free from harm
That they might know our liberty
We wore your flag upon our arm

And oh, the broken dreams
Oh, those Grey Men's schemes
Oh, The Covenant
Hmm, they broke: with me

I've been a zero; I've been a hero
God knows how; I carried on
We sing your songs; you don't sing ours
So tell me: who's the lonely one?
We wore your flag upon our arm
To keep the yearning free from harm
That they might know our liberty
We wore your flag upon our arm

You go your way; I'll go mine
Something tells me; I'll be fine
I've got my Comrades; I've got my love
Still darling: I'm your only one
I wore your flag upon my arm
To keep the yearning free from harm
That they might know our liberty
We wore your flag upon our arm

And oh, my love
Oh, my darling one
Oh, my love
Still feel that flag upon my arm:
I vow to thee my country
I vow to thee, my love
I vow to thee my country
I vow to thee my love *(Repeat)*

Repatriation [7]

They're sending home another plane
Through the rain, the English rain
Those angel lights guide through the sky
Her engines cry, her engines cry
All on board are not alone
I hear them say...
"We're coming home"

From burning sands to waiting hands
They fly so low: they fly so low
Now aching hearts near overflow
With pride and pain: with pride and pain
All on board are not alone
I hear them say...
"We're coming home"

I bless the red, white and the blue
It's what we do: it's what we do
I whisper prayers on softest breeze
But not at ease: but not at ease
All on board are not alone
I hear them say...
"We're coming home"

Come help them safely on their way
Just for today: just for today
Our bugle sounds that higher call
Let banners fall: let banners fall
All on board are not alone
I hear them say...
"We're coming home"

---

[7] Written as Assistant Chaplain-General with the 5th Division: Shawbury 2009

Come wave them off with last salutes
Or what you chose: or what you chose
But can you see that ghostly plane
She's heaven bound: she's heaven bound
All on board are not alone
I hear them say…
"We're coming home"

RAF Lyneham [8]

I have prayed over the coffins of forty-five soldiers
I have carried the safety of thousands in my prayers
I have winced in my heart at our wounded
I have wept at the loss of our dead
I have stood in the rain on parade
I have wished no more planes here to land
I have looked in the eyes of their loved ones
I have sat with their silence and pain
I have saluted the pride of their comrades
I have watched bugle and pipe still the wind
I have marvelled the deeds of the young
I have asked that heaven will take them
I have hoped what this earth cannot yield
I have vowed to continue my duties
I have sought for strength to aid theirs
I have remembered these all once were children
I have given thanks for the day they were born
I have known so many just like them
I have been amazed what they take for the norm
I have sensed the peace of the fallen
I have felt their breath on my face
I have been just a drop in the bucket
I have slept as if grief disappears
I have only been part of their journey
I have been honoured that they're part of mine
I have seen medals and banners and flowers
I have watched it played out on a screen
I have wondered at other men's nightmares
I have met veterans of life and its wars
I have discerned in each: Repatriation
That nothing I know sounds the same
Save the silent flag of this nation
Where the names of our heroes remain

---

[8] Whilst with The Duke of Wellington's Iron Division: Andover 2011

A Good Shoulder, Basra Palace, Iraq

Boy Soldiers

Put on the armour of a thousand battles
Remember the child who played with rattles
Prepare yourself to charge with gun
So long since you ran for fun
The grin you make with fierce intent
So different in your boyhood tent
I can see what you now know
What became of bright Lego?
Comrades take the place of friends
War no place for teenaged trends
Glimpse bayonet flash with foe in sight
Like father taught when lines were tight
Strike now before he has his wish
With firm control to land your fish
But this one won't go home to mother
For her to cook and show your brother
You will never speak with wife or lover

About the day you took another
A guilty man whose tears won't mutter
Broken toys in a dirty gutter
Somehow your regiment proved a winner
But Mum won't call you in for dinner
Brothers-in-arms where courage fell
Leave your torn heart their tale to tell
Those soldiers will not stand again
So different from the ones back then
Each will get a single box
Not like when they came in lots
Shiny colours in Christmas socks
Now harder days when men draw-lots
Used to sleeping in army cots
Letters and prayers for wives and Tots
Those children somehow keep alive
Those safe free days when you were five
Today your battle to survive
Draws on days, when you learned to thrive
Your playground became a battleground
Your game of TIG a burial ground
Then someone says, "I think we're done"
With no more battles your all is numb
Back to the child who sucked his thumb
Your loved ones wait by Runway-One
Military ways have seen you through
Civilian ways have purpose too
Your fighting-team were "Chosen Men"
Now they like you must love again
I doubt your dearest can ever know
All you had to undergo
Put your toys back in their box
Turn the key and seal the locks
Its Christmas Time you are not alone
Your children glad to see you home
Safe beyond the Combat Zone

© West Byfleet 2012

Coldstream Guards [9]

Lay up your Colours
But not your dreams
Remain true brothers
Keep what this means
    Endure through life
    Where others fail
    Engage with strife
    And don't turn tail
Leave Battle Honours
In this place
Sniff out the Conners
Of shifting face
    Carry memories
    Near and far
    Forgive old enemies
    Sooth healing scar
This regiment
Will now march on
No sentiment
Will stall you long
    Three hundred years
    With more besides
    Come dry your tears
    And take great strides
The war drum attends you
One last time
Things found true
Here march in rhyme
    Swords unsheathed
    Make last salute
    Armed guards recede
    With gleaming boot
Scarlet and gold
For the Guards of today
Each crimson fold
Your hearts hold sway

---

[9] With The Household Division: Laying up of Regimental Colours at Doncaster Minister 2012

      Like blankets soft
      On sleeping souls
      Thoughts held aloft
      On prayerful poles
We dare not fail
To earn our rest
Details entail
We beat our best
      Leave sacred things
      In sacred hands
      The bugle sings
      Your next "Last Stand"

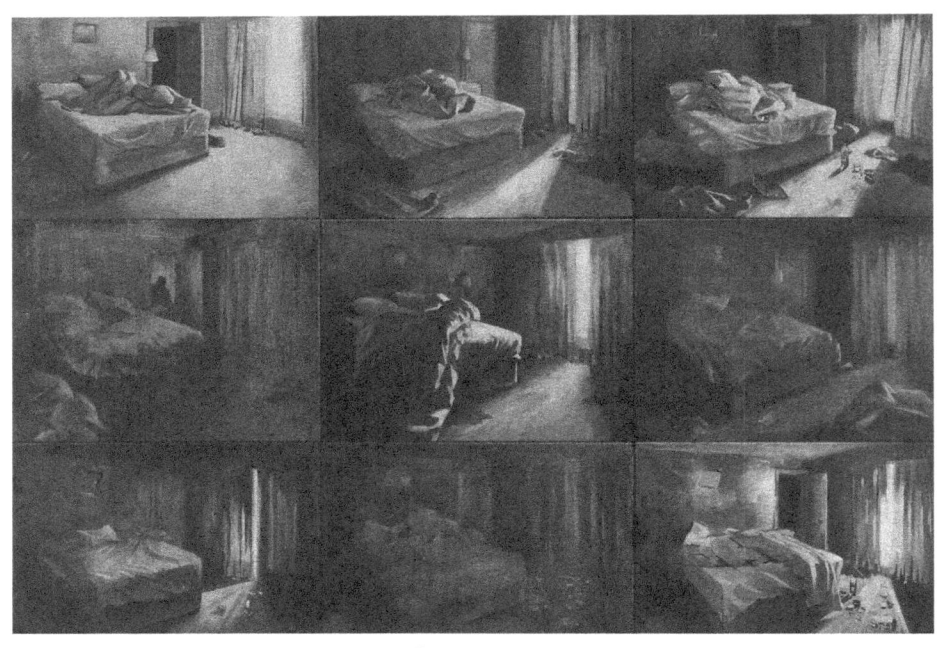

Sleepless.
A study on the effects of Post Traumatic Stress Disorder

London [10]

Standing alone in a crowded street
So many pass my weary feet

Placing hands on a running wall
To steady reality before I fall

Am I the only human left?
Why does my heart feel so bereft?

Or am I the alien, and they the norm?
The man whose fate was long foresworn

My life invisible receives no glance
Just living out my second chance

Now with the world 'off centre' turn
Others' sorrows inward churn

Overwhelmed by all I've seen
Will this heart prove evergreen?

---

[10] Written in Room 100a Grand St Ledger Hotel: Doncaster 2012

Al Basrah, Basra City

Earth [11]

This world is such a sleepy place
Fragile as the loveliest face
Rainbows shattered by jagged rain
Sunbeams burst with conquering flame

This world destroys with little trace
Tattered strands of handmade lace
Savage silence twists the knife
Razor winds discerning life

This world has one redeeming grace
When love seeps through the human race
Bleeding hearts all fire and ice
Scorching through pretence of 'nice'

This world will put you in your place
Laugh to hear you make your case
Watch the Dodo's sad demise
Or strive to see the Phoenix rise

---

[11] Coming towards the end of my time as Assistant Chaplain-General 3rd Division: Andover 2012

Annual Appraisal [12]

Did you come here to serve?
Or merely to observe

When others write or speak of you
Dictating what is true

Do you fight on in silent song?
Determine where your steps belong

Avoid the spoiler's winnowing score
The plight of others to implore

Or do you writhe to know your fate
Oblivious to the poor man's gate

Not just for you this flesh and breath
A selfish man finds only death

"Get over yourself'. The Irish say
Indifference builds a better day

---

[12] Assistant Chaplain-General 3rd Division: Andover 2012

Poet [13]

Unwritten poems linger near
For a quiet hand to scatter fear
With pen on board to sail the gap
Correct mistakes while bow-waves lap

Construct a wind-chime of random words
Gladly fiddle with shapes absurd
Let stillness tingle on spinning breeze
Welcome dear its playful tease

Restful scrump assorted notes
Su-struck thoughts come clear their throats
Fleeting chances sighing weave
Where wooden ships lost souls retrieve

Happy sad cautious free
Live each moment eternally
Rejected commended weak or strong
Fragile suspended through right or wrong

Contradictions making sense
Rarely sitting on the fence
Assembling pieces folding rhymes
Splitting thoughts discerning chimes

Hearing too what does not sound
Makes the audible more profound
Structures speak of bigger things
Assembled pieces hinting sing

Learn passing phrases from heavenly choirs
Heed warning of approaching fires
Rebuild the confidence that others stole
Reclaim your light from each black hole

---

[13] Still with the 3rd Division: Andover 2012

Companions [14]

Walk and talk with God
As simply as a friend
Where saints in dreams have trod
All things broken mend

Between the rock and a hard place
We stride not quite in time
In profile glimpse his founding face
Complete his heavenly mime

A different god would have given up on me
A very long time ago
Priesthood was his gift to me
Despite the Me I know

Pacing still The Bobby's Beat
Unending Parish Rounds
From barrack square to Balkans' heat
Life in my notebook sound

All my strength to come this way
Carrying vows from long ago
"Thanks a million." I am bound to say
To the dearest hearts I know

---

[14] Still serving with the 3rd Division: Andover 2012

Burnham Abbey [15]

Pockets full of silence
Gathered from the floor
Stillness lightly looms immense
Behind each sheltered door

Reaching down past fingertips
To keys that brought me here
Recycled coins mindful flip
Holding breath so near

This is no place for fiddling
With finger, thumb or hair
There is no trace of fumbling
When tracing patterns rare

Tiny women mighty pray
Hush the gathering storm
What on earth brought me this way?
What love their hearts conform

Red, raw, real and true
This veil upon my heart
They guard a path for me, and you
Buy time to play my part

---

[15] Serving with the 3rd Division: Andover 2012

The Dubliner – My late father as a teenager in World War Two
Wearing the uniform of a radio officer in the Merchant Navy

The Dubliner [16]

My Father's medals speak back to me
For these he crossed the Irish Sea
    What became of childhood friends?
    What beginnings brought painful ends?

---

[16] Based at The Guards' Chapel with The Household Division: written at West Byfleet 2012

He lied with others about his age
As an Englishman filled in the page
    One more name for the Merchant Navy
    But still his family called him "Davey"
Serving first with the old Home Guard
Studying Morse and the Nautical Yard
    Then sailing the Atlantic in Convoys packed
    Where dwindling U-Boats still attacked
Japan's vast Empire challenged next
Where Kamikaze left men vexed
    POWs all skin and bone
    Made his heart a falling stone
The cruelty of spiteful nations
Kept good men at lonely Stations
    Haunted by what his enemy could do
    Hating what they made us do
And what became of wartime friends?
Hopeful souls who met theirs ends
    Suits grown cynical through so much war
    Declared "No Jobs" the final score
But the Dubliner stood his ground
Believing that his case was sound
    "You're Irish aren't you?" the pinstripe said
    "What of it?" spoke Davey so long past dread
"You're lucky to be alive" the Englishman jibed
Dad turned the tables determined to strive
    Through many long years he earned his days
    Carrying the mark of snobbish ways
Ireland would not welcome his like
"You've made your choice so get on your bike"
    They thought it was just an Englishman's war
    But my father saw it was everyman's war
He met my Irish wife and daughter
Planned one last voyage across the water
    But the angel of death on retirement eve
    Of all life's burdens did my father, relieve
He never again saw the land of his birth
No wonder his medals contain such worth
    Now Dublin sleeps in English soil
    Free at last from earthly toil
Who would believe that the peace we enjoy
Was built by such an Irish boy

Wazha Pa Wazha (Shoulder to Shoulder), Afghanistan
British soldiers play football with Afghan comrades, shortly
After a devastating "Green on Blue" on Remembrance Day 2012, where
Walter Barrie was shot dead by an ANA soldier
and comrade in arms, whilst teaching him how to play football.

Blue Collar [17]

The Working Man, near breaks his back
To build a home, not just a shack
Almost never answers back
Made then saved, the Union Jack

He pays a fortune to watch his team
Sees them drive a dream machine
Rarely has a selfish dream
Cheers them on with bursting scream

The bus he rides is just the same
Where boys once played, down street and lane
Since first he learned to write his name
He coped by following "The Beautiful Game"

---

[17] With The Household Division: written at West Byfleet 2013

Life governed by the factory clock
The wife who proves his daily rock
Children his most treasured stock
Rolex players all tick tock

He held strange ground with bayonets fixed
Outsmarted even Hitler's tricks
With comrades proved a ready mix
Not like a job where "Off at six"

His kind, guard palaces, in Scarlet and Gold
Make Jubilee, a story told
Helmets plumed, with armour bold
Household Honours that can't be sold

It's time to know, to show again
These: rarest; finest, fighting men
Ceremonial like Big Ben
You can tell the time by fighting men

Yellow card, red card: referee's whistle
Shamrock; rose; leek and thistle
Working Men of bone and gristle
Blues and Royals with Life Guards bristle

Their officers raised by different rules
Trained to sort the wise from fools
Swords and hearts like old time duels
Different games from different schools

Bound together with Working Men
Better together than days back then
Stand together 'till heaven knows when
Waiting for Orders from Number Ten

Win or lose; through every weather
These are the men that stick together
Others may reach the end of their tether
Medals teach when not to be clever

Wounded men hushed by the grave
Of every hero they couldn't save
Praying hearts like banners wave
Feel the need to drink and rave

Chaplains drink the sad man's jug
Act like fuses in a plug
Contest with those who pull the rug
Fill with wine the soldier's mug

Our drinking-well, kept safe from hell
Our deepest roots, where none can tell
Our heaviest thoughts, our sweetest smell
Our hearts consort, our souls foretell

These Working Men, have seen the end
These officers, have proved their friend
These Guards by deeds can comprehend
These bonds of peace and war, defend

Football tickets sweep the street
Winds attending marching feet
Working Men know well the beat
Come through victory and defeat

Cheering fans in football stand
Troops safe home, make all feel grand
Off Duty, loves a different band
The Working Man who crowns this Land

Day and Night, I've seen him homeless
Memorials to when he proved a bonus
How strange my heart should feel the onus
The 'Debt of Honour' that he has shown us

De Mob [18]

Pack my bags by the Barrack Gate
Time and comrades seal my fate
Ripened well but much too late
Every kindness wipes the slate

Soldier On with heavy song
Even when the days are long
Don't retire from fighting wrong
Find the Shire where I belong

The Thin Red Line runs through my heart
I stood with those who played their part
The world sees Gold and Scarlet smart
But I have prayed where feelings start

So rare to meet the Selfless Streak
Walking down your Average Street
I have known what few will seek
Exhausted slept where boundaries meet

My uniform is put to bed
Along with days when heart was lead
Clothed, housed, paid and fed
But now I face a different dread

Starlings scroll like Writer's quill
It was raining then and it is raining still
They paint the Sunset with such thrill
Descending down against their Will

There burns a light that won't go out
An Eternal Flame that will not shout
Cauterize the wounds of doubt
Bags of tea deserve a spout

---

[18] With The Household Division: written at West Byfleet 2013

Medals proud for all to see
Some look like a Christmas tree
Hide in drawers each memory
Find heart to be Good Company

What will replace the years we serve?
Embattled days of wit and nerve
Soulful soldiers still deserve
More than just a Learning Curve

Parade [19]

The walls of England
Are flesh and bone!
To Gold and Scarlet
Their hearts are sown

Comrades trusted
With their name
Friendships form
Their pride and pain

They have been to places
Where no one goes
Medals shine
From nightmare holes

Memories march
No more afraid
Apprentices
Who learned their trade!

This spectacle
Shows how it's done
Since Waterloo
When Freedom won

The Union Flag
Is still held high
Streaks of blood
Through English sky

Colours guarding
Crown and Sword
Beasts and men
Take history forward

---

[19] With The Household Division: written at West Byfleet 2013

Ghosts of Empire
On parade
Saluting Honours
For which they paid

The wind is full
Of old and new
The soul enjoys
Its own curfew

Stay with love
That never came home
Befriend the heart
Forever alone

Be quick to sniff
The spine of straw
Learn to live
Through peace and war

Lead follow or
Get out of the way
These men have bought
Your brand new day

See the dark-light
In their eye
Veterans know
The reason why

For some they are just
A steppingstone
But to me they speak
Of all things home

Breaking notes
On dying breeze
Because of them
We stand at ease

Choose your Creed
Or none at all
Build a bridge
Or build a wall

Keeping safe
This Land of choice
Shades of silence
Where all have voice

Restless dreams
May seep regret
But England has promised
She won't forget...

Sandhurst Chapel [20]

Prepared to be where few men stand
I traced the altar with my hand

Softly layered this bed of sleep
Which end should I lay my feet

An empty tomb to tempt my head
Dare I rest where he once bled?

St Michael's sword upon the cross
Victory rises through my loss

Candles wait like angels tame
Names cut deep await love's flame

Clergy chant each handpicked word
But in this place my all is stirred

They ping pong light familiar prayers
But I am drawn to winding stairs

Small steps bringing heaven in view
A father's love in richest blue

"My son" held here just out of sight
To calm his dreams through raging night

If England lives then who can die?
Yet adult tears refuse to dry

Indifferent prayers drone on and on
Herd the blind through Evensong

At last with pride they say Amen
Leave me with these slaughtered men

---

[20] Behind an altar and half hidden by stairs, is a memorial window to a fallen son: written at West Byfleet 2013

Letters show they braved their part
While Regiments were torn apart

Remembered here in wood and stone
The chalice holds their flesh and bone

Broken silence: crumbled bread
Help me tuck my boy in bed

Woolwich [21]

Flimsy petals of loving power
Drooping guard the barrack tower
Fresh emotions rainbow sprayed
Sore hearts built this barricade

So many nations living near
Feel the chilling bite of fear
Those who act in black and white
Do a wrong and think it right

The ruins of a young man's life
A broken throne for every wife
Falling tears to cleanse the knife
Bugle Call suspending strife

Will any good rise up from this?
Is there something still amiss?
Handshake phone call nervous kiss
Second-Guess a scene like this

Scarlet tunic empty proud
No Drummer Boy to please the crowd
Some things can't be said out loud
Silence proves a lasting shroud

Is this breaking making Britain?
Not all by the Vision smitten
Some it seems are all for quitting
Which solution will prove fitting?

Commandeer when Love draws near
Breach the wall of Hate and Fear
What others loath we must hold dear
Standing true from front to rear

---

[21] Following the murder of a British Soldier on the streets of Woolwich: written at West Byfleet

Why did those men become so mean?
Offending God insulting Queen
Humble people stand between
Wake to make a brighter dream

Armistice [22]

The world had heard enough
It was time to smooth the rough
    Ragging guns and men
    Lumbered home again
So unlike before
The once familiar door
    Silence feels the knock
    The gulp of battle-shock
Dare his heart go in?
To all that might have been
    Will bleeding memories mend?
    Will haunted eyes offend?
Can hands worn limp with strife?
Confess upon his wife
    Gentle as a child
    Before The Mad went wild
Can naked heal his clothes
The uniform that knows
    Can midnight sheets adjust?
    Fields of bone and rust
No Treaty here entwined
No Armistice of mind
    So silk so soft his dreams
    A bed of poppy screams
Loving living while we grieve
Molecules of hope retrieve
    Remembrances of broken days
    Condolences in morning rays
Did ribbons paint a peace like this?
Pay the price of Love's first kiss
    Silence churns beneath my breast
    Soil confirms our sons at rest
Sunlight wakes the catacombs
Academics write their tomes
    Joy revives where Freedom lives
    Still surprised when hurt forgives

---

[22] Approaching my last Remembrance Sunday as an Army Chaplain: written at West Byfleet 2014

Weathered prayers built in layers
Mark the end of splitting hairs
  Why they tried and why they died
  Opens wounds so deep and wide
Here I sit where mothers cried
Wondering if my God replied

Another Beautiful Day in Shaibah, Iraq
White memorial crosses stand guard over memories and sacrifice,
in a foreign 'field' in Iraq.

Clueless [23]

It is not kind or wise to claim the high moral ground
Or 'Lesser Mortals' - hound
For we are all human with golden seeds and faults
Priceless treasure in broken vaults
We win or lose we hurt and heal
We take for granted Love's next meal
We get it right we get it wrong
We stay too short we stay too long
We hold things back we rush right in
We wrap our tears in Heaven's grin
We understand but then we don't
We raise our hand but then we won't
We save it all then let it go
We hide away and make a show
We can't forget the things we should
We miss the grain that guides the wood

---

[23] With The Household Division: written at West Byfleet 2014

We seek a crown beyond our size
Miss the Life before our eyes
We shed the blame that long was ours
Abandon stars for earthly powers
We see the clues but not the crime
Wind our watch on borrowed time
Exasperated like a saint
Holding on while others faint
We live with ringing in our ears
Gather roses for our tears
We think we've seen it all before
Can't believe we're on the floor
Theologians ought to know
When to rush when to slow
Instead the mother with her pram
Guards her heart just like a dam
The soldier's widow walks through rain
No one sees her burning flame
Her broken pieces hold the clue
To precious things forever true
She wears a cross fit for a queen
Wide-awake while others dream
Her love holds tight this frightened world
Heals the sky where prayers are hurled
Unspoken kindness fills the leaves
Hands her Windfall from the trees
And we the clueless pass her by
Cannot look her in the eye
In case we learn the reason why

A Moment's Respite – For The Queen's Own Gurkha Logistic Regiment at Shailbah

Island Race [24]

I love this land of little ships
No caviar: just fish-and-chips

Where others sink: we somehow swim
What others start: we often win

The Armada came: to burn our laws
But little ships: destroyed their cause

They mocked our men: at Agincourt
Until we changed: the Art-of-War

Napoleon thought he had us beat
But Nelson sank their finest fleet

---

[24] With The Household Division: written at West Byfleet 2014

At Waterloo it was the same
We held our ground: in England's name

The Retreat-from-Mons: gave bullies hope
But English blades cut binding rope

Buying time: with brain and steel
Holding back: the jackboot heel

Dunkirk saw us: down-and out
But little ships restored the rout

Another day we would return
In time to make their hatred burn

Through Norman fields: so like our own
With Saxon shields: of flesh-and-bone

Longbow prayers: strike hard the foe
English hearts: make panzers slow

Factories, shops and family farms
Rendered safe: by English arms

Our caring ships: brought liberty
Daring wolves: beneath the sea

Since then so many foreign wars
Have made the wisest weep and pause

The courage of our bravest men
No different to those days back then

The spirit of our women folk
Enough to make a grown man choke

The language of the Common Man
Finds the gaps: where children ran

Little ships: bear England's name
Heal her pride: and ease her pain

From woodland hills: to sliver streams
A land of golden timeless dreams

Where strangers talk: and children play
Winds of freedom: cool the day

With battles won: and batsmen caught
We prize each home: and ruined fort

Castle towers: with memories lined
Stories pour: where rich men dined

Oars demand: that all pull hard
Muscles weighing: every card

Little ships: will sail again
When England needs: her Chosen Men

Empty tokens: cannot stand
Upon this green and pleasant land

With the pen: and with the sword
Our progress was: forever forward

But now the world: eludes our grasp
Glories sparkle: in the past

Shadows: of our former selves
An island race: upon the shelves

Where now the men: who shook the world
With thoughts and hearts: and flags unfurled

Poets, priests and politicians
Happy feasts: and good decisions

No matter what: the nations say
Little ships: can save the day

Rank [25]

In fear and awe
Of manmade rank
Who to blame
Who to thank

In truth they barely
Knew your name
Perhaps enough
To keep you tame

In time you learned
To call their bluff
By gentle ways
You bore the rough

In hope of better
Days to come
You kept the Faith
And kissed the Sun

In love with tripping
Over dreams
Nothing real
Is was it seems

In fact the soil
Beneath my feet
Does more to make
My life complete

In turn my roots
Are deeper now
Than those with rank
Who claim know-how!

---

[25] Preparing to lay down my rank as retirement approaches: written at West Byfleet 2014

In every moment
I have known
A richer fruit
Is quietly sown

On Patrol – The 2nd Battalion the Rifles, Sangin, Afghanistan

Remember [26]

That was then
When long ago
Hidden seeds
Began to grow
    Careless words
    Thoughtless dreams
    Lives that litter
    Magazines
What the Hell
Is going on
Feel the silence
In the song
    Little changes
    When we pray
    Human nature
    Has its way

---

[26] I did my share of UK Repatriation Ceremonies at Wooten Bassett and elsewhere. After four years my final tally of fallen soldiers reached fifty-two. This poem came to me after my last Repatriation: written at West Byfleet 2014

Farmers know it
More than most
Burning pride
With morning toast
    Ragged seasons
    Strip the trees
    Chilling hearts
    With savage ease
Feel the burden
Of it all
Feel the angels
Rise and fall
    Heartbeat sticking
    Clogged with glue
    Contradicting
    What I do
Quieter: quieter
Everyday
Thoughts like lovers
In the hay
    Fewer words
    Is what we need!
    Let the silence
    Warm the seed
Who planted what?
Or why and when
Where gone the boy
I knew back then
    He ran through fields
    Climbed begging trees
    Cut his face
    And tore his knees
Friends like flowers
Bloom and die
Colours changing
With my tie
    I used to risk
    Those handlebars
    But now I tire
    Of boozy bars

I used to reach
And touch the sky
But now the world
Adjusts my tie
>   I used to smile
>   In every weather
>   Storm and sun
>   Held me together

My father freed me
From barbed wire
But now I am snagged
On wild desire
>   Fallen soldiers
>   Silent loom
>   Rows of coffins
>   Fill the room

Union Flags
Times fifty two
Like boyhood blankets
That I knew
>   Sleeping safe
>   Where none can harm
>   Stealing apples
>   From the farm

The sleepy deer
The sneaky fox
Will not go near
Pandora's Box
>   It quietly beats
>   Within my chest
>   Beside the things
>   I know are best

Planting seeds
Every day
The only proof
I came this way

The Reunion [27]

The saddest angels I ever saw
Sat with soldiers home from war
Respectful silence filled their wings
The violence of eternal things
None could answer why or how
The Devil thought to take a bow
The memory of Heaven lost in Hell
Drinking from a poisoned well
The eyes of men look straight ahead
Cling to comrades brave and dead
Angels staring at the floor
Veterans of a different war

---

[27] After visiting the church of St Mary Magdalene in Latimer. It had silent war memorials and beautiful mosaics of angels: written at Latimer: 21 January 2016

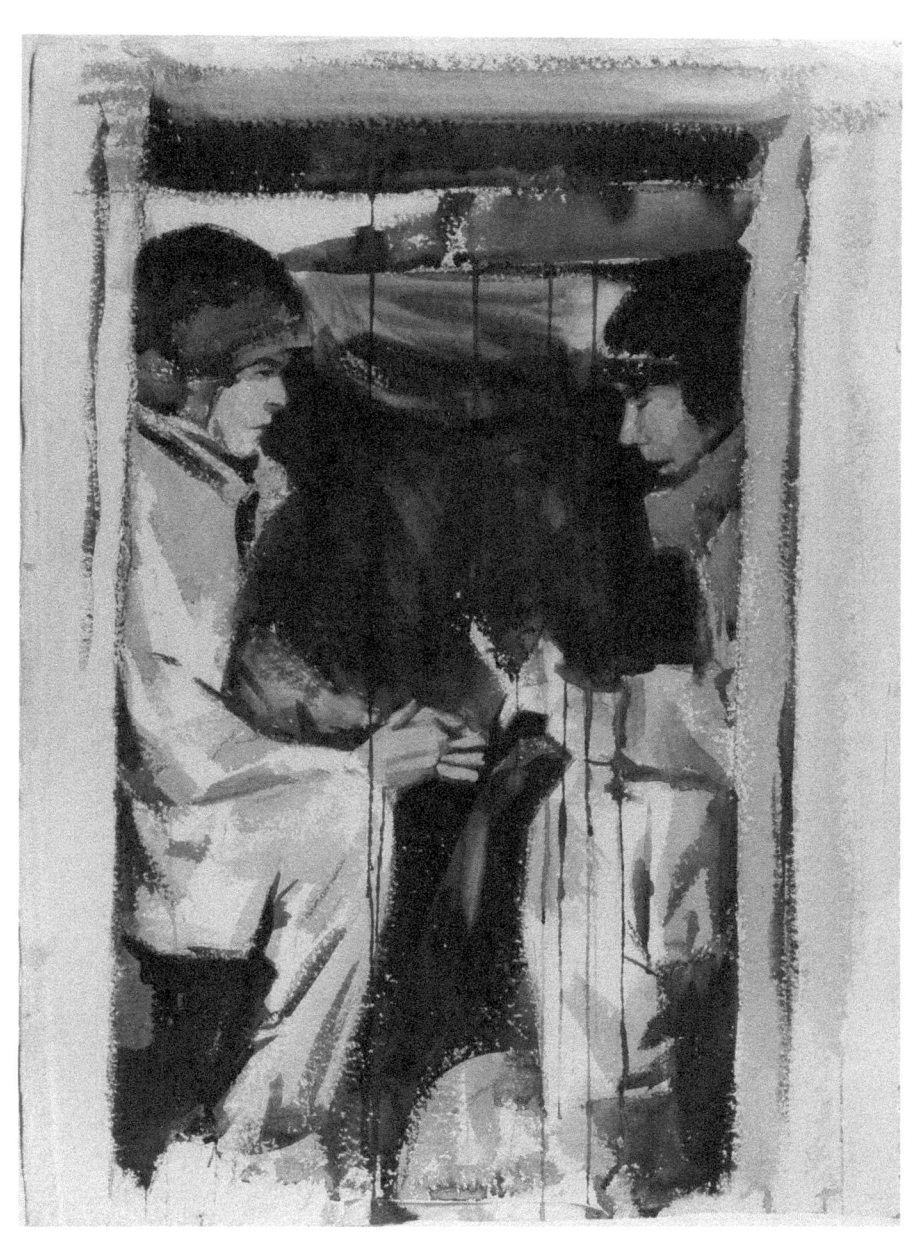

'Waiting in a Warrior' – Basra Palace, Iraq

Homecoming [28]

Travelling companions
Out with battalions
Home through canyons
Rally the stallions

Through fields of hate
The hours were late
Clean the slate
Or seal your fate

The drums of war
Are back in store
But like we saw
There's always more

Soldiers know
What doesn't show!
Brothers grow
Where none should go

Tattoos collide
So deep inside
Memories hide
As if a bride

Some resist
The broken fist
But dreams persist
And won't desist

Ribbons match
The tattoo scratch
Close the hatch
Pin the latch

---

[28] Coming to terms with transitioning from military to civilian life: Twickenham 30th January 2016

Finally home
Escaped the zone
But still the Drone
Disturbs their bone

*Taqalla Baraye Zenda Mandan (The Struggle to Survive) -
Afghanistan*

Embers [29]

It's my turn to sleep in the bottom of the boat
With unspoken feelings stuck in my throat
The storm has passed and I am on my way
Silent timbers rock and sway
My eyes are closed but I see his face
As he tugs the oars with a steady pace
Carried safely to I know not where
All my cares blow through his hair
Alone with others just like me
Hiding on the Syrian Sea
The weight of all that brought me here
Falling like a salty tear
Taste the dreams that fill my soul
Breaking bleeding healing whole
Breathing out and breathing in

---

[29] My parish was about to host an art exhibition by the remarkable Arabella Dorman. Her experience of war zones and concern for refugees is well known. She liked this poem so it became a prayer card for visitors during the exhibition: Twickenham 2016

Tides of thought make heaven spin
Between the near and distant shore
I rise and fall, just like an oar
Remembering those so far from home
Who seek the peace we call our own
Portraits hung with fading prayers
The ghosts of children on empty stairs
Embers of a better day
Framed with more than words can say
Embers rising into flame
Leave the darkness tired and lame
Still the oars must creek and grind
Splashing water through my mind
The world is full of refugees
Christ is rowing on his knees

Flanders' Memorial Garden [30]

The birth of life was followed by
The death of baby boys

The founding of the Church by
The smashing of their toys

The hush of heaven's breath by
The most disturbing noise

The hope of every day by
The things that fear employs

The birth of every prayer by
The weakening of our joys

The raising of the dead by
The rushing that destroys

The kindness that can heal by
The cruellest kind of poise

The words that bring it home by
The it that so annoys

The dawning of the light by
The shadow that decoys

The broken bread and wine by
The hunger that is coy

The coming of the kingdom by
The memory of Troy

---

[30] This Great War Memorial Garden was installed in 2014 outside The Guards' Chapel. It marks the British Guardsmen who died liberating Belgium and contains soil from seventy-four battlefields. I was honoured to bless that soil and write the Order of Service and Dedication: Twickenham, December 2017

The silence of true wisdom by
The fool who shouts ahoy

The purest given reason by
The things that must alloy

The victories of war by
The heart that is La Croix

I am what I am [31]

I am a sailor for Mary
A soldier for Christ
An Airman for angels
Concealing the price

I am a gypsy for Jesus
No roots but my own
A tumbling weed
In search of a home

I am more than they say
Less than they know
A man making footprints
In mad melting snow

I am what I am
So never you mind
The best of my future
Is trailing behind

I am broken in places
That others know well
A warrior healing
Who never will tell

I am coming to terms
With all that I've seen
The joy and the pain
The truth and the dream

I am listening to souls
That struggle to speak
Learning their language
Becoming complete

I am done with demanding
What no one can give
Preferring the wisdom
Of live and let live

---

[31] Almost two years since retiring from my restless life as an army chaplain: Twickenham, January 2017

I am hoping the answers
Belong where they should
With a man on a cross
Who did what he could

Where Watchmen wait [32]

The ghosts of soldiers guard the town
In case they let the living down
They never sought to make a name
Instead they played a different game

The lady with the lamp stands near
With tender flame to banish fear
Attending those who gave too much
Healing with her homely touch

They seem so calm in winter clothes
Dressed in grey from head to toes
Experience has made them bold
Only the living feel the cold

She watches all with eyes of pity
Silent in our noisy city
No casualty escapes her gaze
Or soul that longs for better days

Comrades formed from captured guns
Fought the fear that overcomes
Bear the marks of battles born
Colours battered bruised and torn

She with them will rise again
To fix the weary hearts of men
Sooth the wounds that linger deep
Dress the dreams that will not sleep

Guardsmen standing strong and true
Do what others will not do
For God and country: cross and crown
Still they guard Old London Town

---

[32] I had just been to a Veteran's lunch in London. Afterwards I found a large statue in honour of Florence Nightingale. It was flanked by statues of British Guardsmen: written at Twickenham, December 2017

The Veteran's wife [33]

I thought you were done with medals
The Veteran's wife enquired
didn't we agree
they never really suited you
and they were no friend
to me

The last one came in the Post
For Long Service and Good Conduct
They even added a Bar
But you've already been gone
Three years
And we did over twenty six
Yet nobody has given me a medal
Even if I wanted one

So why bother to have this last one
Mounted with all the rest
I only wish they saw you
when I've known you
at your best

Hang them all if you must
and hang them all I say
you are better off without them
living day by day
it's about the here and now
not what you did then

Where are all those comrades
forgotten just like you
No one comes to see you
No one has a clue

---

[33] In my day, officers were not entitled to the *Long Service and Good Conduct Medal*. After I retired they changed the rules. Luckily I met the criteria, applied, and after a year, I got my gong: Twickenham, November 2018

But I'm glad that you're not sulking
or simply giving in
like a man without a cause
who reads about the wars

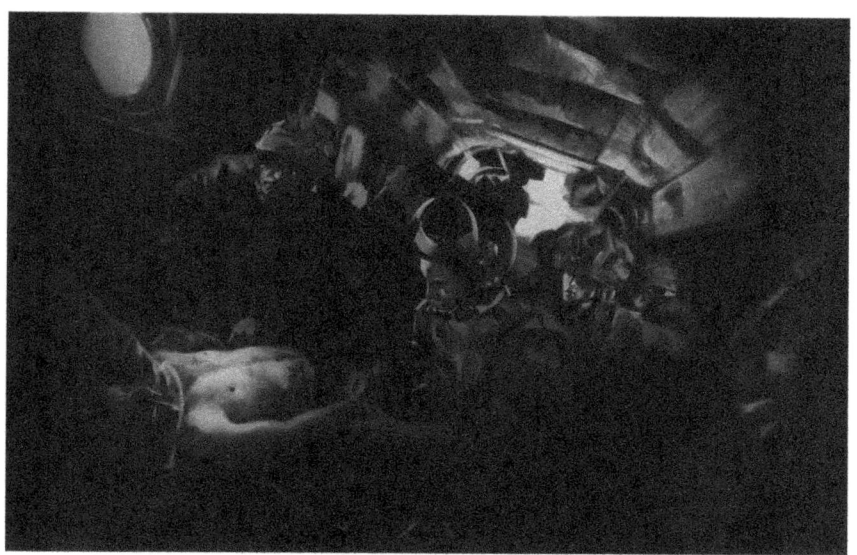

The Medical Emergency Response Team (MERT) –
These extraordinary Medics fly to the point of contact, and extract the wounded, often under enemy fire. Note the female Medic.

Sky Taxi [34]

The bodies of my enemies
Are riding in the sky
Carried to the sunset
By blades that spin on high

My comrades did for them
Before they did for me
We are children of the dawn
From a land across the sea

I'm a pilot in a war
That no one here foresaw
I'm the son my parents love
I'm an angel from above

---

[34] I once spoke with a young army helicopter pilot. His experience of war challenged his humanity. Yet affirmed his Christian faith. I have never forgotten him. My own story became blended with his: Twickenham, 29 March 2018

The apache in my hands
Brings death and life and hope
A warrior understands
The memories that choke

We fingerprint their dead
Their faces in my head
I weep within my tent
All my courage spent

Bullets fly like prayers
Tearing through the layers
The heroes at my side
Thank me for the ride

I look for bread and wine
Where the broken hearted dine
Go fix my smashed machine
But not my silent scream

If it's all the same to you
I think that I am through
There's something I must do
It's time for something new

I miss the cruel and kind
The sighted and the blind
The medals and the flags
The history that drags

I will never be the same
Or remember every name
Feet firmly on the ground
I fly without a sound

Great War days [35]

They say this war is a lovely war
Because this war won't cause more
So off we march with horse and drum
Far away to fight The Hun
Our women cheer and watch us go
There's just so much we've yet to know
Children run where shadows wait
Playing games in fields of hate
Here in the dying snow
Here where the cold winds blow
And love is the last to know

We're not the men we used to be
We've seen things that none should see
We've said prayers no saint should know
Like burning flares where brave men go
Our comrades wait through fear and fire
Our leaders plot and late conspire
You'll find the living with the dead
The whistle screams inside my head
Here in the dying snow
Here where the cold winds blow
And love is the last to know

They were great days in the Great War
We never saw their like before
1914 seemed like a dream
1915 was hard and mean
1916 near broke my heart
1917 the Yanks took part
Come the end both foe and friend
Began to think they'd never mend
Here in the dying snow
Here where cold winds blow
And love is the last to know

---

[35] My personal tribute to all who came home and those who never did: Twickenham: August 2018

What on earth did you expect
Just come home and reconnect?
The normal world you fought to save
Cannot see your living grave
The mirror listens to my soul
Remembers when my life was whole
Captured by my silent stare
Vacant as the morning air
Here in the dying snow
Here where the cold winds blow
And love is the last to know

What will they say in a hundred years
Will poppies guard our secret tears
The strength we never knew we had
The love of friends to make us glad
Dusty medals in a drawer
Flags that feel the wind no more
Bury me with horse and drum
God forgive the things we done
Here in the dying snow
Here where the cold winds blow
And love is the last to know

Dawn over the Shaat al-Arab, Basra, Iraq

Where soldiers dream! [36]

I have been where soldiers dream
Felt the feelings unforeseen
Far from family and friends
Where we served for different ends
To smell his fear, pride and pain
To stand with him in heat and rain
To pray for him when no one will
Because we trained his hands to kill
To carry on without a song
Until you've lost where you belong
To wonder at the days you knew
When the world was bright and new
Silent medals keep the score
Closed to every open door
Kept within that private place
Along with every passing face
The bugle sounds but once a year
Remembering those whose names are dear
The pipes will wail on weeping wind
They call to all who loved and sinned
The seed of things we should have known
Rests where poppies long have grown
Do angels bind what will not heal
Do saints and sinners share their meal
Do flowers on a soldier's grave
Help the living to be brave
Does the sinking of the sun
Say another race is run
Or give us hope that come The Dawn
The sun will rise on all who mourn

---

[36] Remembering and Remembrance: with the British soldier in mind: Twickenham, 27 August 2018

Where none can see [37]

Last night I dreamt of you
The things we used to do
When the rules of day do not apply
Firelight captive in your eye
The shadows in our dancing hearts
Hint the moves that love imparts
The silent shifting sliding dreams
Bold as shy supporting beams
The memory of things begun
The treasury of healing fun
The lost concealed within the found
The joy that whispers not a sound
We dare to trespass
where none should go
Longing for the afterglow
We share the candle
And the flame
Weld ourselves
A different name
Timeless flying falling free
Tumbling with expectancy
Landing soft in pillowed arms
Deep within such secret charms

It was so surreal yet utterly real
So much more than life's next meal
Like a simple banquet of bread and wine
You are the one for whom I pine
Where pain and pleasure
Walk hand in hand
Into the wilds
Of a distant land
Where poppies grow
And rivers flow
Whispering things
That none should know
I mourn you now and always will

---

[37] On Retreat at Walsingham: 2019

You are my heart my hurt my thrill
I walk with you where none can see
Renew our love on bended knee
It is the love that never dies
The one beyond all earthly ties

My keepsake is my emptiness
the open wound I can't confess
The things you touched
And loved so well
Bring comfort to my private hell
Including me your last heirloom
Caressed within our private room
I am living proof of what we were
The constant things that daily stir
Forget-me-nots are breaking ground
Bringing strength I have not found
Colours bursting proud and true
Remind me when
Our love was new

So I wait where none can see
Where hearts can wander free
Alone among the crowd
At home among the proud
Where a kind of mercy lingers
Wind through hair like fingers
Where the kiss of winter rain
Sooths away my pain
Where memories form a wreath
Smiling through my teeth
Where someone calls my name
But it's never quite the same
Where angels on the street
Guide my weary feet
Where shadows of despair
Float upon the air
Where the kindnesses of strangers
Keep pushing back the dangers
Where every breath is you
Affirming all that's true

Where no one understands
Your medals in my hands
Where no one comprehends
Our beginnings and our ends
Where no one knows the love
that rests within my glove
Where all we are together
Is mountain, sky and heather
Where my tongue cannot express
How more can seem like less
Where the shift from heal to toe
Can make the feelings grow
Where all we've yet to be
Is safe where none can see...

Chief Joseph [38]

I am all in arrears
Way beyond tears
The feelings won't come
It's the numbness that steers
We fought and fought bravely
We did what we could
Cut down in our prime
Like a tree in a wood
The songs that we knew
Were noble and true
They came from the silence
That knew what to do
The old ways like water
Have slipped through my hand
Along with the memory
Of all that we planned
No longer a stranger
To the white man's ways
In peace or in danger
We hear what he says
My lance and my shield
My head and my heart
My love is a field
Where friends never part

---

[38] Written in Twickenham: February 2019.

The Last Bugle [39]

I have twice handed in my uniform
To those I loved and served
I carried those clothes and insignia
As much as they carried me
We picked each other up
We stood side by side
Through dizzy dazzling days
Only to lay each other down
Parting Company forever
Such it seems is the way of things
We give our all to certain things
At the expense of other things
But in the end
We have to let them go
And move on
In order to carry the weight of ourselves
And those we love
For the strength and agility
We had when young
Will also let go and move on
To other things
One uniform is a distant memory
The other is slowly being eaten
By moths who seek the light
But without understanding
Dancing like clamouring fools
On the window of my soul
At least I do not burn them
As a naked flame would surely do
There are mothballs now
Strategically placed
In the last uniform
I so carefully wore
Driving back the invading moths
That were eating: my memories
My pride and my honour
Slowly digging up the path
That I had trod
A path becoming invisible
To where I now stand
Or those with whom

---

[39] Written on a train from Twickenham to Worcester: 28 March 2019

I live and serve
In a higher cause
Than I have ever known
Before...

Safe Return, Royal Green Jackets, Basra Palace, Iraq

Where heroes passed *

Gaps widen with the years
Drain the well of unseen tears
Outside everything stays the same
Inside no one hears your name
Depression seeps into your soul
It seems your life is swallowed whole
You feel at home on broken ground
Where normal men cannot be found
The marginalised misunderstood
Become a thing that's understood
Paralysed in thought and deed
When will self from self be freed

Locked inside an invisible room
I think too late, speak too soon
The rising tide of self obsession
Only adds to my depression
Powerless, without a key
No one seems to know or see

I cannot bend or break the spell
A prisoner in my private hell
I push the door that has no locks
Feel the hole within my socks
Fear my heart is turning hard
Every inch becomes a yard

Once I knew what I stood for
In times of peace in times of war
Once I stood where heroes passed
Felt the world was spinning fast
But now the world is turning slow
Little things have stole the show
Why so hard to find my way
Know the thing to do or say
When to fight when to run
Face the sadness in the fun
Chasing prayer between the trees
Casting breath upon the breeze

Today my sleep has paid the toll
Lonely thoughts go for a stroll
The emptiness so deep within
Shows me where I must begin
Virtues that I thought were mine
Glisten in this un-dug mine
Darkest secrets wrap around
Starless midnight floods the ground
Sparkling seeds of greater wealth
Speak of love that lives by stealth
For the darkest day in time must yield
When sunlight frees the golden field

* Written in Twickenham: 2019.

The Dance, Afghan schoolgirls dance as a sandstorm gathers in the foothills of the Himalayas, Central Afghanistan

Something New [40]

Shadows of my former self
Dance around me like an elf
And yet it seems I walk alone
My only friend a mobile phone
Images fill heart and screen
With all the places I have been
The granite of my parents' grave
Makes me wonder what we save
Will the cold etch deep my name
Defiant sunlight warm the same
Will fingertips trace weathered lines
That show the dates of former times
Will flowers placed with loving care
Confirm my heart had learned to dare
Will things that give my soul no rest
Finally cease their endless jest
Will stone-like stillness strip the bark
Reveal the love that lights the dark
Will they show how much I hid
or just enough to lift the lid

---

[40] On a Residential Clergy Course at St Columba's House: Woking, 04 June 2019.

Through the eye of the storm [41]

I have looked in the face of a perfect storm
The kind that claims it is the norm
It smiles to keep you off your guard
Undermines your own backyard
Preys and plots behind your back
Works to knock you off your track
Protests it never can do wrong
Will not hear a different song
Craves attention night and day
Twists everything to have its way
Makes everything about itself
Eats its way through every shelf
All the others are to blame
A wolf that plays so very tame
Tries to cast a lasting spell
Always first to kiss and tell
There's darkness in its cheery heart
A shadow poisoned like a dart
Controlling and manipulative
Drains your will to love and live
It makes you feel you just can't cope
Ties endless knots around your hope
Believes the world will fall apart
Unless we feed its hungry heart
So I break free in search of right
Step with joy into the light
Look for souls with just one face
The kind that love without a trace
They delight to see the other thrive
Just so glad to be alive
They only wish my greatest good
Walk with me by lake and wood
They catch each other when they fall
Guard the manger and the stall
See my hunger and my thirst
Build the best: ware down the worst
They see the way to get things done
Give the devil cause to run

---

[41] Composed in Twickenham and Burnham: 16th & 17th August 2019

They sense the songs that sift through me
Words that rhyme with hill and sea
They pray the poet in my breast
Will one day find eternal rest
That I should live with elves and men
Gives me cause to say Amen
That I have known what can't be shown
Gives me strength to walk alone
I'm tired of those who say they're good
In the way my saviour never would
I ache and mourn for what we are
The love that gives despite the scar

Song Writing [42]

When you build your silence
Into a song
It sounds in the heart
Like a faraway gong
It holds together
The notes that you sing
Causing the bells
In your mind
To ring
It waits like a siren
Drawing you near
Before it unleashes
A smile and a tear
It breaths into words
A spirit that's true
You know that it's there
When that spirit comes through
Like the wind on your face
When the sun warms your bones
Or when soldiers return
Like ghosts to their homes
Yes the song full of silence
Comes from deep underground
Where un-dug treasures
Have yet to astound
For the song full of silence
Marinates every note
Causing a lump
To appear
In your throat

---

[42] Written in bed after a 'long long day': Twickenham 5th October 2019

Above the City, **Herat, Afghanistan**

Notes

Come walk with me   Page 05

The Queen's Royal Lancers famously took part in *The Charge of Light Brigade*. Their distinctive Skull and Crossed Bones 'Cap badge' is unique, as is their "*Death or Glory*" Motto. The regiment were already stationed in Osnabruck when I became their chaplain. I was newly promoted to 'Major'. Family walks through strawberry fields were common as was the sight of wild poppies. Germany seeped into this poem even though my thoughts and feelings were about Britain and the wars that destroyed her Empire but not her families or her farms.

A Bosnian moment   Page 06

This small country is roughly the size of Wales. I got around in an army Land Rover. My driver was a young soldier form Brixton. Every Monday we set off from our Base and covered much of the country before returning at the end of the week. We found town after town and village after village, utterly or partly destroyed. We also saw School playgrounds empty of children. Yet often close by was an unmarked mound of earth where most of them were buried. The different racial groups were like matter and antimatter or oil and water. Instead of burying their differences, they had decided to bury each other. I arrived roughly one year after the war ended. Yet the whole place seemed like a stale bonfire or an open crematorium. This poem helped me to draw on deeper things in order to deal with the depths of human depravity. In those days we were loosing roughly one soldier per month, in Mine-strikes or an RTA.

Epitaph   Page 07

In the summer of 2001 my family and I arrived in Northern Germany. My new job was as Senior Chaplain with the famous 'Desert Rats'. At that time they were officially known as 7th Armoured Brigade. Our barracks had been home to German soldiers during World War Two. Trains regularly stopped outside it to 'drop off' Jewish prisoners who then walked the final one and half kilometres, to Belsen Concentration Camp. The rest as they say is history. Part of that history would be a girl called Ann Frank. Our brigade deployed to Kosovo. It was my second time there. What I saw in Kosovo, combined with the impact of Belsen, and caused me to write this poem. Before I knew it we were posted back to England.

The Warrior

I could not believe that our new home would be in *Bagdad Road* on Salisbury Plain: that seemed like a military joke in bad taste. By now I was a 'Lieutenant Colonel' with 43 Wessex Brigade. Their recognition flash is a Saxon Wyvern on dark blue background. Apparently that had been the battle flag of *Alfred the Great* who withstood *The Danes*. But it was also the flag flown by *King Harold*, who was unable to withstand the Normans. It is ironic that in Normandy during World War Two the brigade fought so bravely and so often that they became known as *'The Fighting Wyverns'*. The Germans who faced them came up with a different nickname: *'The Yellow Peril'*. During my time with them, many full and part time soldiers were fighting in Iraq and Afghanistan. I felt very much that the 'warrior tradition' of our islands was still alive: even though some were dying or receiving life-changing injuries.

George

I tried to imagine St George as an Army Veteran walking through the streets of London. He was on his way to Temple Church in order to visit the tombs of fallen knights. I walked with him and our reflections mingled in shop windows. But when we got to the church it was locked against us.

I am afraid this experience happened to me. I had to settle for being outside and looking up at the famous pillar. On top of it are two Templar knights, on one horse. This beautifully expresses *The Buddy System* that is so central to army life. Simply put: you do not leave your comrade behind, especially if he is wounded or unhorsed.

Finding the church closed was for me something of a distressing experience. Around that time I had become interested in the original Templars and read much about them. So much so that I became a Novice with a modern Christian version of the Order that takes its inspiration from those first Templars. OSMTH has over seven thousand members in seventeen countries. I was seeking some extra spiritual support to get me through my military duties. Nothing in civilian life came close to my needs as a military chaplain in the modern world. So this personal pilgrimage meant much to me.

Finding the doors closed against me only served to reinforce how I felt at that time. On the other hand, being outside the church whilst looking up at those two knights served to lift my moral and spurred me to carry on. But the whole experience left me feeling outside the church in every sense of the word. I always explained to others that, "I am a Christian priest in military service..."

Suddenly however, it seemed that the church was hanging on to our fallen comrades whilst leaving people like me standing out in the cold with no access to those I had come to honour and remember. I am afraid I still feel this about the national church that I have served for most of my adult life. It seems to me that the military man must leave his sword at the gate, even if it is a spiritual one, before he is allowed to enter the church that he defends and kneel down to remember his fallen comrades.

I too am now a veteran whose reflection has changed and civilian clothes have replaced my military ones. One day I will return to Temple Church and complete what was begun in 2008. Hopefully when I am ready: the moment will also be ready. Ideally it would be good to sneak in and out without being detected.

In the meantime, I am convinced that in this world there are still dragons to be slain. So many wrongs that need to be righted and so many things that need to be defended because they are good and proper and right true.

Heal the Flag Page 13

In the summer of 2007 they promoted me to 'Full Colonel'. Off I went to Shropshire to become Senior Chaplain at the Divisional level. I quickly discovered that The 5th Division had a long and distinguished history. During the Great War they took part in most of the major battles. That earned them the nickname of which they were rightly proud: *The Fighting Fifth.*

There were several small teams of chaplains in my care. They took it in turns to deploy to hot and dangerous places. I was full of admiration for them. I reflected on their comings and goings. Those prayerful thoughts mingled with my own homecomings from Bosnia, Kosovo and elsewhere...

The result was this song. I sang it to the pupils at Hereford Cathedral School in early 2010. The pupils responded strongly to it. The school got in touch and invited me to make a charity CD. This was achieved via a local I-tunes record producer. My folk song was turned into something a bit more like a pop song. But I went along with it because the charity concerned allows military children to stay in a Fee Paying School if a soldier parent is killed on active duty.

All my heart said *yes* to the project. I think the CD is still available via Amazon UK. It goes by the title of this poem: *Heal the Flag*. Also on that CD is the following song, called *Repatriation*. I am glad we raised money for a worthy cause and that I never took a penny from those songs in that format.

Repatriation Page 15

An I-Tunes record producer listened to more of my songs. He even got me to do a demo album with him in March 2010. During the breaks he asked me about my life and work as an army chaplain. Eventually we got on to the Repatriations that kept coming my way. He said I spoke with passion about those experiences and suggested I tried to write about them.

I normally write the tune and the lyrics at the same time. But this time the words came without the tune. I emailed the lyrics to him. His strong response compelled me to work on a tune. The finished song went onto the same charity CD mentioned above. Once more, my folk song became a pop song. But I went along with it for the same reasons. Both songs kind of belonged together after all.

The following year I was posted to the 3rd Division. Sadly the chaplain who replaced me in Shropshire proved to be the last to hold that appointment. The Division was disbanded and *The Fighting 5th* is sadly no more.

RAF Lyneham Page 17

The UK Repatriation Ceremonies began at RAF Brize Norton, then they moved to RAF Lyneham. I was *in* from the beginning. I prayed for it all to end. I never thought that it would indeed end at RAF Lyneham and Wooten Bassett, only to move back to Brize Norton, where it all began. We were not 'off the hook' for a good while yet. Sadly, more families were to suffer what too many had already suffered.

By this time I had been promoted to full 'Colonel' with oversight of thirty-eight chaplains in four teams. There was always one team in Iraq, one in Afghanistan, one about to deploy and one recovering having come home. They were a splendid bunch and some of them needed medical support after what they had done in support of others. Together we ministered to 25,000 soldiers and their families. As for the fallen, I tried not to keep count. I knew that if it built in my mind then I would not stay the course. But when we got a new general he asked me how many I had dealt with.

He was clearly taken aback when I said. *"I have no idea"* because he told me to find out and let him know.

So I went to the desk officer at MOD Chaplains in the hope that she had kept a log of chaplains like me. That is when I discovered that my tally of fallen soldiers had reached forty-five. It was a 'sinking moment' and provoked this poem. In future I kept my own log and updated it, when duty called.

Boy Soldiers   Page 18

In April 2012 my family arrived in the village of West Byfleet. I reported for duty at the Household Division where I was interview by the Major General. He received me in the same office that had been used by *The Duke of Wellington*. The general sat in the same chair at the same desk that had been used by the great man: and I felt like I had come home to something wonderful. Just in time for two Olympics and a Royal Diamond Jubilee. My boyhood toy soldiers had come to life: even as they were facing death.

I think this poem was the beginnings of me digesting the Repatriation experience, and perhaps, my whole military 'career' to that point. For retirement was just over two years away and somewhere out there, was a Christian Community that would welcome me, as its parish priest.

Coldstream Guards   Page 20

Regimental Colours look like flags to civilians. But they are even more special than that... to those who follow them, with every breath at their command. Like soldiers, like life itself, Colours wear out and need replacing. The old Colours are traditionally laid up in a spiritual place of safety. A moving ceremony accompanies this event.

This poem began beforehand as I anticipated the significance of what was about to happen. The ceremony took place in Doncaster Minster where Bishop Peter Burrows received the Colours and gave us his blessing. I will never forget being inside the Minster as the lone deep drum sounded like a heartbeat, whilst the Old Colours were carried up the aisle. When they stopped near the altar, the drum also stopped beating and it seemed to me like an old friend had died, as that beating heart finally stopped. That dramatic moment allowed me to go home and complete the poem.

London Page 23

Whilst in Doncaster, for the 'laying up' of those Regimental Colours: I was staying at public expense in a local hotel. In my room I reflected on a recent experience whilst walking in London near to Wellington Barracks. It went like this: I suddenly became dizzy and wobbly on my feet. It felt like the world was a ship lunging from left to right, then spinning like a globe, until I could no longer stand unaided.

I remember reaching out with my left hand to a low brick wall and used it to steady myself, until the feeling passed. That took several minutes, and at one point I could no longer see the world around me. What must passers-by have thought of this man with a dog collar clinging to a wall, with shops and offices all around?

Thankfully, the feeling eventually passed, as the spinning world slowed down…

Gradually I stopped crunching down and unravelled myself once more: until standing upright. I became aware that both hands were clinging to the wall. First I released the right and then the left: followed by slow deep breathing. Only then did I feel safe to step forward and re-join the world around me. I remember feeling embarrassed and a little ashamed that for a moment, I had literally lost my balance, and place, in the world. The feeling of defenceless vulnerability was overwhelming. Arabella Dorman worked out what this poem was about, when I shared it with her. Even before I did.

Looking back, I think all those fallen soldiers, grieving families and broken chaplains, was finally catching up with me. I literally could not stand on my own two feet any longer. Mercifully those experiences are now behind me. But this poem remains.

Earth Page 25

So many times I have stood by a grave and said *"earth to earth, ashes to ashes, dust to dust."* At the time of this poem, my days with The 3rd Division were nearing their end and it was time to reassess what dies, what survives and what rises from the ashes. In our bereaved and wounded, I saw the love of families and comrades stitch together, what war had torn apart.

The Union Flag is such a delicate flimsy wrapping with which to adorn the coffin that carries a fallen soldier. And yet its colours seem so strong, so untarnished, so complete and intact.

Those bittersweet Repatriation days broke and healed with the same breath: I will never forget how brave; are those who love: or how splendidly the RAF honoured the fallen and their families.

Annual Appraisal Page 26

My duties with 'The 3rd Division' included care and oversight of thirty-eight full time army chaplains: ministering to twenty five thousand soldiers and their families. At the time this amounted to a quarter of the British Army. I was tasked with writing their annual reports and took that duty seriously. I also believe that a Christian priest should care more about what is in his heart and his diary: than what is in his annual report. Over the years I met one or two who just did not get it and were quick to defend their annual appraisal. A few would phone chaplaincy headquarters on an annual basis to find out where they had come on that year's Promotion Board.

To me this still feels deeply at odds with being a priest because it carries the scent of self-interest. I tried to play it differently. Indeed for my last five or six years: my annual online 'wish list' stated clearly my preferences. So when senior officers looked me up before beginning to write my Annual Report, they would see my submission loud and clear. *"I do not wish to be promoted"*. And yet every year as a 'Full Colonel' chaplain, I was recommended for promotion to the role of Deputy Chaplain General. It carries the 'equivalent rank' of Brigadier. I am glad it never happened.

Anyway, my last job in the army was about to start. So I put in this poem what I could not say directly to those concerned. There is no point contending with those who fight for themselves rather than for others. Thankfully this was not the majority.

Nonetheless getting it 'out of my system' in this way, allowed me to move on. It also allowed me to double-check with myself that I had never once defended my own annual appraisals: even when I knew that what was written was wide of the mark and devoid of insight. I preferred the content of my heart and diary to those flimsy bits of paper that are already years behind me, and nowhere in sight. Today as parish priest they are meaningless and without currency.

Poet   Page 27

It dawned on me that I was 'self-medicating' every time I wrote a poem. It was not something I chose to do. But something I needed to do. This piece was trying to understand how and why I write. It was also about coming to terms with those unwritten poems that military life never allowed me to start or finish. There was just too much going on. Part of me mourns those uncompleted things.

Companions   Page 28

Reading this after several years, confirms that I was finally beginning to see my life as whole: right back to when I joined the West Midlands Police, on leaving school and home; at the age of sixteen.

Burnham Abbey   Page 29

This special place is home to enclosed Anglican nuns. They have a rota of male and female priests who say Mass for them. They like to have a few military chaplains on that rota and I have remained on the team, despite retiring from the army. In fact I am one of their *Priest Companions.*

The Dubliner   Page 30

In World War Two, my father went to England with his father and brother. The Second World War was in full swing. He was just seventeen and lied about his age. Strangely they put him in *The Home Guard*. There they trained him with certain skills. Those allowed him to move on and become a Radio Officer in *The Merchant Navy.*

Thousands of Irishmen fought in that war. But a neutral Irish Government had a policy of 'No Jobs' for those who fought, alongside the English. Indeed it was not until 2018 that a national Memorial Stone was unveiled in Dublin. It acknowledges the Irish who died in both world wars.

When my father died in 1991 his medals came to me. They have been with me ever since. This poem was my attempt to let them speak for him and those like him.

Blue Collar   Page 32

My time in the army allowed me to observe many things close up. Not least the contribution, of the workingman, to the life and security of our nation.

De Mob   Page 35

I watched others retire from the army and disappear from sight. Once they were gone they were gone. This common occurrence set me thinking about my own retirement: even though I still had two years to go. How would I cover the remaining ground and what would I find when my time ran out?

Parade   Page 37

Remembering remembrance is what this poem is really about. I mean remembering England as a place where remembrance can safely take place and will not be forgotten. At another level it is about the once popular 'Military Covenant' that is supposed to exist between the soldier and the nation.

Sandhurst Chapel   Page 40

There is much to see in this famous chapel. But a curious wander, into quiet unfamiliar corners, can unveil neglected messages and acts of remembrance. Behind one altar is a curving flight of stairs.

At the foot of those stairs is a stained glass window from a father to his son. I was very moved by the quiet, stillness and presence that clung like grieving hands to the window frame, and begged a prayer from each passer-by.

I had returned there to attend a 'Training Day' for army chaplains. Finding a window that I had not noticed before; made the experience worthwhile.

Woolwich   Page 42

I was based at *The Guards' Chapel* in London when these events unfolded. All my training and experience tugged at me to get in the car and go myself. But the burden of leadership means picking up the phone and sending somebody else.

It also means trusting that person to do a good job while you do yours. I did visit a few days later and despatched a second chaplain to assist.

Sometime later, writing this poem helped me to digest the whole sad experience.

Armistice　　　　　　　　　　　　　　　　　　　　　　　　Page 44

My military service was coming to an end so there was time to reflect on foe and friend. This day always seemed like 'The Junior Partner' to Remembrance Sunday. Yet for me it always caused a significant pause in my day. Especially when an enlightened commander ensured that it was commemorated with a chaplain key to his plan.

Clueless　　　　　　　　　　　　　　　　　　　　　　　　　Page 46

The Elizabeth Cross is not well known in civilian circles. But it ought to be. At the height of the Iraq and Afghan wars, Queen Elizabeth 2nd introduced this award.

It is only given to the nominated Next of Kin, when a military person is killed on duty. Its large fist sized cross and the small accompanying lapel cross, are formerly presented to the recipient. How typical of this Queen that such a personal 'thank you' should go from her to those who have suffered so much. Thinking about that and all those repatriations, caused me to think further and harder, than ever before.

For instance, I remember turning up to do yet another Repatriation when an RAF officer spoke to me. We were talking about the 'Duty Generals' who turned up and spoke with the families, more like a father, than a VIP. He remarked that last time one family were deeply moved to notice that the brigadier talking with them was wearing an Elizabeth Cross on his parade uniform. But said not a word about it…

They knew what it meant and were deeply moved that he had suffered like them. I gather he lost an officer son in Iraq or Afghanistan. It was not my place to check the details of the story or the nature of his pain. But he was wearing that Cross and that was enough for the family and enough for me. God bless him wherever he is now!

Island Race　　　　　　　　　　　　　　　　　　　　　　　Page 48

The small ships of these small islands withstood *The Spanish Armada*; triumphed at *Trafalgar*; and even smaller vessels rescued our soldiers, at *Dunkirk*. The same is true of our army. I was thinking of the 'small' man from small towns and even smaller villages. Thanks to them big things have been achieved and may yet be achieved in days to come.

Rank Page 51

During my final months in the army I was beginning to disengage, reflect and look back on the lessons learned. One of those lessons was about rank. In my opinion some wore it badly and carried it like a weapon or a box to stand on.

It was hard to see one or two doing harm with something that is meant to be a force for good. It is certainly not meant to foster any feelings of self-importance or make a Padre more officer than priest.

Remember Page 53

As a boy I fell in with some rum company. They hit on the idea of going to the local golf course and collecting lost golf balls. We got under the barbwire fence and started gathering our prizes. But then a group of male golfers started walking towards us: and my companions decided to run for it. They pushed me out of the way and dived back under the fence to freedom. Before I knew it they were on their bikes and gone.

Whereas I could see that the men were getting closer and one was in the lead with club in hand. I turned away and darted desperately under the fence but the back of my jumper got snagged on the barbed wire. I was in a state of panic and realised there was no escape. I was well and truly trapped. So I looked over my shoulder and saw that most of the men held back. But the lead man kept coming ever closer.

Eventually I looked up; the man stopped and smiled at me: only then did I realise it was my father. He unsnagged me and I smiled back with relief. The tears that were rising in me sank back down to the place where they are stored. No words were exchanged. I got away under the fence and cycled home alone. Those who had deserted me never came near me again.

Throughout my life, other things have snagged me from time to time and strangers have proved friends whilst friends proved strangers. Soldiers and barbed wire fit well in the same sentence. But they do not fit well in real life…

I have seen them snagged on so many things, including death itself. My years of doing Repatriations were finally behind me. My years in the army were about to end. My time for reflecting was increasing. My need to make sense of it all was deepening with poems like this one.

The Reunion Page 56

Almost a year had passed since retiring from the army. I had returned to life as a parish priest. The Diocese of London sent me on a residential course at Latimer Place. I think the aim was to 'teach me' how to be a parish priest. Anyway, I felt out of place with my new peers and knew there was no point in explaining. It was my problem not theirs. The style of worship being offered was not helping: so at one point I sneaked off for a quiet moment on my own, to the church we had been using. Namely, *St Mary Magdalene*.

I knew that *The Knights Templar* had a special devotion to that saint because she was the first to see Jesus, raised from the dead. So things started to feel a bit more military for me as I sat there in the silence like a soldier on guard duty, or a medieval Knight, keeping a private silent vigil.

Then I noticed the quiet names on the war memorials and finally the beautiful mosaics of angels. Suddenly I could see how it all joined up. It was just a matter of how you look and why. But also who and what you are; and where you have been. The words came quickly and quietly. A reunion of sorts had taken place.

Homecoming Page 58

The second of February 2015 is when I was Inducted as Vicar of All Hallows Church in Twickenham. When the powers that be, began suggesting dates, I asked for this date because it was *Candlemas*. The symbolism and beauty of that Christian Festival; seemed to me to be the perfect way to resume my ministry as a parish priest. I was also privately aware that *Candlemas* is when my parents were engaged.

As a family, we discovered quickly that life in army quarters is very different to life in a vicarage. My first anniversary of being in the parish was just a couple of days away. I guess I was privately pondering what that first year meant. It was also a way of marking the map. In order to see how far I had travelled, down the road of transition that leads, from military to civilian life.

Embers   Page 60

In the autumn of 2016 our parish welcomed the artist Arabella Dorman and her remarkable body of work. We raised around two and half thousand pounds for the charity *Medicines San Frontiers.*

Over a three-week period nearly two thousand people came into our Christopher Wren church. It was a wonderful and memorable experience for all concerned. This poem was written shortly before the exhibition.

Flanders Memorial Garden   Page 62

In the First World War around fourteen thousand British Guardsmen lost their lives in the battle to liberate Belgium. The Government and people of Flanders chose to fund a Memorial Garden at *The Guards' Chapel* in London. They gifted a quarter of a million pounds towards the project. In Belgium, school children collected soil from seventy-four battlefields where British Guardsmen lay buried. Seventy-four sandbags were then taken on a gun carriage to *The Menin Gate.*

There a military 'handover ceremony' took place and the precious cargo was taken to a Belgian warship. That then sailed for England and came up *The Thames* where *Tower Bridge* opened to let it through. It was then put on a British gun carriage and escorted by mounted troops of *The Household Division* through London. It eventually came down *The Mall*, past Buckingham Palace and finally into *Wellington Barracks*. There it stopped on the parade square with its escort, before coming through onto *Chapel Square*.

Once it was safely in place, I was handed a seventy-fifth sandbag containing soil from all seventy-four battlefields. It was my honour to bless it and see it placed into the new *Flanders Memorial Garden*.

The Order of Service was written by me from scratch because there was nothing on the Church of England shelves that came anywhere close to this event. Present was our Queen, with Prince Philip the Duke of Edinburgh.
Also present were The King of the Belgians, and our own Prince William, the future king. This would be my last public duty as an army chaplain. The following week I was interviewed for the parish in which I now serve.

I am what I am   Page 64

By now I was more settled in my surroundings as a parish priest. The healing I sought for others: I was unwittingly seeking for myself. So many experiences were now at the service of my parishioners. Yet old skills and old habits had to be applied in a new way. Listening to people in a parish is different to listening to people in the army. I cannot explain it. It just is.

In both contexts, I found myself looking in the same place, for straight answers: to my misshapen questions. Proof if any were needed that being a priest in the army is essentially the same as being a priest in the parish: those who say otherwise are wrong in my opinion for they have failed to grasp that the Christian priesthood is a medicine, that can be universally applied.

Where Watchmen wait   Page 66

I am lucky enough to be Chaplain to *The Pen and Sword Club*. Its four hundred or so members are those with journalistic skills who have served with or alongside British Armed Forces. I sometimes manage to attend their monthly lunch clubs in London. On this occasion I had just left the lunch venue and found myself looking at a large statute erected in honour of military heroes from the Crimean War.

On the train journey home to Twickenham I used the notepad on my mobile phone to write this poem. I later submitted it to the official army magazine of *The Household Division.* Happily *The Guards' Magazine* liked this poem and published it in 2017.

The Veteran's wife   Page 67

The medal referred to in this poem is supposed to be officially presented by a senior person. In my case the local postwoman delivered it to the vicarage where my wife signed for it because I was 'out and about' in the parish. The sentiments expressed reflect my pastoral encounters with many wives and loved ones who shared in the burdens of military life. They really should get something when it is all over. As for my wife, I doubt she wants or needs anything, from those days. Nonetheless, this book is dedicated to her and those like her.

Ski Taxi   Page 69

I think that 2011 was the last time I spoke with this young officer. Yet what we shared has remained with me. Finally several years later I found the words to try and express what war demands of men like him, with faith like his.

Great War days   Page 71

Remembering the end of *World War One* is something that our nation did well in 2018. In our parish church we were well prepared for *Remembrance Sunday* and the Centenary Commemorations that would mark the end of hostilities in November 1918. But I felt a deep need to make my own contribution…

The result was this poem. It was added to the final Order of Service. I submitted it to *The Guards' Magazine* for their consideration. They published it in 2018 just in time for Remembrance Sunday. I felt very pleased that they had found my poem worthy on this special occasion.

Where soldiers dream   Page 74

This poem quickly followed *Great War Days*. The Armistice Centenary Commemorations were proving to be something of a magnet: pulling together my thoughts and experiences about my working life to that point.

Where none can see   Page 75

This poem was written over a period of three days. For me it arrived as a strong candidate for this book. So I admitted it as a late addition to the manuscript.

I believe it speaks for itself and needs no further introduction. Except to say that it ends on a hopeful note….

Chief Joseph   Page 78

Towards the end of *The Indian Wars* few tribes remained at liberty. One of them was *The Nez Perce*. They had an old treaty with the US Government and had always lived in peace with the whites. Yet at short notice they were told to get onto the Reservation or be regarded as 'Hostile'. Most of the tribe did so. One group was attacked. Women and children were killed or raped. A second group refused to abandon their way of life. Both groups joined together. Their plan was to go north into Canada and join Chief Sitting Bull. He and thousands of Sioux warriors had been given political asylum by Canada after *The Battle of the Little Bighorn*.

Chief Looking Glass led the group that had been attacked. *Chief Joseph* led the group that had refused to go onto the Reservation. Together they led eight hundred people. They had just two hundred warriors. The rest were women, children, the elderly and the blind. For one thousand eight hundred miles they out-shot, out-ran and out-manoeuvred two US Armies. They fought thirty-four battles and skirmishes and inflicted heavy casualties on their pursuers. They were always outnumbered at least two to one. The two Commanders opposing them were battle-hardened veterans of *The American Civil War*. One was a general: the other a Colonel.

The Indians had traditional weapons and rifles. The soldiers had rifles and artillery.

Eventually, just thirty miles from the Canadian border the exhausted Indians were caught between two armies. It was the dead of winter, with falling snow and deep snowdrifts. The soldiers fired artillery at women, children, warriors, the blind and the elderly. For three days the battled raged. The women 'dug in' with kitchen utensils.

It was a heroic last-stand for a doomed way of life. *Chief Looking Glass* was killed early in the battle. *Chief Joseph* was elected to take overall command. Finally they were out of ammunition. Some wanted to fight on. But Joseph was filled with compassion for the courage and suffering of his people. He felt he could ask no more of them. He felt he had 'failed' to protect them. So with just eighty-seven warriors left he resolved to surrender.

At the end of that last day, he crossed the battlefield towards the enemy. His best warriors walked with him, each with a hand upon him. The opposing armies looked on as he drew closer. The soldiers and officers were stunned to see that the traditional clothes and blanket that Joseph was wearing, were full of bullet holes.

There was a brief exchange, the senior officer promised 'safe passage' back to their traditional homeland, with no prosecutions. Joseph accepted and made a surrender speech in his own language then handed over his rifle. His words come to us from the Indian scouts that served with the soldiers. Even now I find them very powerful and memorable:

> "Tell General Howard I know his heart. What he told me before, I have it in my heart. I am tired of fighting. Our Chiefs are killed; Looking Glass is dead, Ta Hool Hool Shute is dead. The old men are all dead. It is the young men who say yes or no. He who led on

the young men is dead. It is cold, and we have no blankets; the little children are freezing to death. My people, some of them, have run away to the hills, and have no blankets, no food. No one knows where they are - perhaps freezing to death. I want to have time to look for my children, and see how many of them I can find. Maybe I shall find them among the dead. Hear me, my Chiefs! I am tired; my heart is sick and sad. From where the sun now stands I will fight no more forever..."

With that he handed over his rifle. The enemy gave him until the next day for his people to come towards the soldiers. The Indians dragged this out, allowing those who were willing and able, to slip away towards Canada. Joseph and those left behind went with the soldiers the next day. They were the majority. He soon discovered that they had been lied to. Instead of going home they were being deported three hundred miles away from the place they loved: at first on horseback but then by train. Joseph was a celebrity with the whites. In fact the newspapers called him *The Red Napoleon*.

They also remarked that this tribe took no scalps but had acted honourably and humanely throughout the conflict. Even to the extent of Indian women going out on to the battlefield to treat wounded soldiers, as well as their own warriors. Whereas the history of *The Indian Wars* carries many true stories of US soldiers deliberately targeting women and children. Even to the extent of shooting low into the wigwams when attacking Indian villages. In order to cause casualties among those who were sheltering. Familiarity with Indian ways meant that the US Army knew full well, that some of those Wigwams were used as nurseries for children, hospitals for the sick, or as 'care homes' for the elderly. Whereas the warriors; were 'out and about' in the thick of the battle.

On the journey into exile, Joseph had opportunity to speak to local politicians. He did so with great skill. He was now using his tongue to fight for his people. Instead of his rifle:

"I have heard talk and talk, but nothing is done. Good words do not last long unless they amount to something. Words do not pay for my dead people. They do not pay for my country, now overrun by white men. They do not protect my father's grave. . . . I am tired of talk that comes to nothing. It makes my heart sick when I remember all the good words and all the broken promises. There has been too much talking by men who had no right to talk. Too many misrepresentations have been made, too many misunderstandings have come up between the white men about the Indians..."

On arrival at the final Reservation they were reunited with the rest of their tribe, many of those had embraced the Christian faith at the hands of white missionaries. Joseph was so called because his father had embraced Christianity. When white folk asked him why he had stuck to *The Old Ways*, instead of accepting Christianity, he gave an answer that moved my heart and moves it still, because it shames and shakes Christendom right down to its basic foundations: I wish his ghost would appear at *General Synod* within *The Church of England* and utter these haunting words:

> *"We do not want churches because they will teach us to quarrel about God, as the Catholics and Protestants do. We do not want to learn that. We may quarrel with men about things on earth, but we never quarrel about the Great Spirit..."*

Those sad and prophetic words were not arrived at easily. Joseph had been baptised into the Christian faith but became deeply disappointed by it: as practised by none Indians. Members of his tribe referred to the bible as *The Book of Heaven*. Yet the father of Joseph ended his life equally disappointed and incensed by the white men. Finally the old man burned his copy of *The Book of Heaven* along with *The American Flag* that he had once treasured. No doubt all of this had a deep impact on the younger Joseph, who had led and defended his tribe with such courage and integrity.

It was this Joseph who championed the suffering and the cause of his people for the rest of his life. More than half of those taken into exile died from neglect, wounds and disease. Of the eight hundred people he had started with only around two hundred and seventy survived on the reservation. I can only imagine how the rest of the tribe responded with relief and grief. A terrible injustice had been committed. A peaceful tribe who had never made war on the white people had been provoked into a flight for freedom. Never again would they see their ancestral homeland.

They say that praise from your enemy is praise indeed. General Sherman famously marched through Georgia in *The Civil War* and brought *Hell* with him. He is also famous for a conversation with a 'Red Indian' man who acted as a Scout with the US Army. The man pointed to his heart and said in his broken English. *"Me good Indian"* To which the General replied. *"The only good Indian is a dead Indian."* Sherman certainly had no love for the Indian race. He was content to hold Joseph and his people in inhumane conditions. And yet when asked by newspapers about the war with *The Nez Perce* he had nothing but respect for his former enemy:

> *"The Indians throughout displayed a courage and skill that elicited universal praise… they fought with almost scientific skill, using advance and rear guards, skirmish lines and field fortifications"*

When Joseph died in 1904 he was just sixty-four years of age. His doctor said that the cause of death was, *"a broken heart."*

During the months of war, he had ordered his warriors not to take scalps and not to torture the wounded. Such was his standing with them that they obeyed. Even though they knew that soldiers do not take Indians as prisoners. This makes Joseph a moral hero as well as a military one.

His tribe in particular was unlike others that the whites had fought. For instance, during *The Apache Wars* the torture of prisoners and scalping, were common. Also after *The Battle of The Little Bighorn* it became clear that scalps were taken and torture was common. No wonder then that Joseph and his people stood out in the public imagination, as being humane, even in the middle of a war that should never have happened. For the white nation, Joseph stood out among noble Indians as perhaps the noblest of all. It is no surprise to me that this moral hero, went onto become a political one. Indeed his death was front-page news, in the newspapers of his former enemies.

When I look back at my own military service, I reflect that Joseph fills a gap in the training and culture of Christian and military leadership. For me he is a powerful example of *Compassionate Leadership*. I do not see much of that in politics. I was privately on the receiving end of it from a few senior officers on *The General Staff*. Unfortunately, in my case, I received almost none of it from the more obvious candidates. No doubt others had a more positive experience. I hope that most found me compassionate, for I tried my best and gave of my best. Either way, those days are gone, and I cannot change the past, even if I wanted to.

Finally, Joseph was well named at baptism, with the name of an Old Testament hero who had watched over his people, whilst living among strangers. Yet it was his Indian name that lingers with me. It means simply this, *thunder rolling down the mountains.*

I feel it best, to end with his words, rather than mine:

> *"Whenever the white man treats the Indian as they treat each other then we shall have no more wars. We shall be all alike—brothers of one father and mother, with one sky above us and one country*

around us and one government for all. Then the Great Spirit Chief who rules above will smile upon this land and send rain to wash out the bloody spots made by brothers' hands upon the face of the earth. For this time the Indian race is waiting and praying. I hope no more groans of wounded men and women will ever go to the ear of the Great Spirit Chief above, and that all people may be one people..."

He also said: *"It does not require many words to speak the truth".*

Further reading:

Chief Joseph & The Flight of The Nez Perce: *The Untold Story of an American Tragedy.* By Kent Nerburn: Published by Harper Collins, New York 2005.

The Earth is Weeping: *The Epic Story of the Indian Wars for the American West.* By Peter Cozzens: Published by Atlantic Book, London 2018.

The Last Bugle   Page 79

I had arranged with my two brothers to meet for lunch in Worcester. It was my day off from the parish. It was also the third anniversary of our mother's death. The previous evening I spoke with my wife and decided to book a train. Rather than go by car. My plan was to read and relax. Instead my notebook came out early in the journey and the words bubbled up inside me. I realised that this was going somewhere and that some sort of closure on my military service was forming on the small pages. More than twenty-six years in army uniform was being condensed and distilled.

It also became clear that my pen was excavating through the layers of my life. Soon the remnants of an older uniform came into view. It was a civilian police uniform like the one that I wore for six years, during the nineteen seventies.

As the train carried me through the green sunny English Countryside, I did the sums and concluded that I had spent a total of thirty-four years in uniform. I suppose that suggests strong threads of continuity. Yet I sometimes feel that I have changed more times than I care to remember. Those who have worn uniform will know what I mean.

Finally, I find myself serving as a parish priest. In that role I have ended up where my journey began. You see I was baptised as an infant in a parish church by a parish priest. Now I baptize infants in a parish church as a parish priest...

Where Heroes Passed   Page 81

I started this poem in late May and finished it in early June. Whilst going about my parish duties and errands, it kind of followed me around. It kept demanding attention until it was done. It took me to dark thoughts and feelings. Yet it also showed me the path to something golden. Something for which we are all looking. I hope this poem helps anyone who has wrestled with depression. Whether caused by military service or by other means. This poem is also about the difficult task of transitioning from one way of life to another. We all have to do it in different ways at different times and for different reasons. We have to let go, in order to take hold of something new.

Something New   Page 83

Four years and four months as vicar of a wonderful church with some splendid people. Surrounded by a vibrant and diverse community. In my time here I have grown to know streets and places but also hearts and faces. Suddenly an email informed me that all full time priests aged fifty-eight or older, can attend a three day Residential Course about Retirement. At sixty-one this was not on my mind. But it seemed wise to get an early look at what the Church of England thinks I need to know before I get there. So I went on this course and I am glad that I did: for a number of reasons. I had been planning to work until the month before my seventieth birthday. But discovered on this course that the average retirement age is currently sixty-eight. Time will tell.

Either way, the Course was giving me time to stop, think and reflect on my life journey. Collating this book has definitely been a matter of laying down my military life once and for all. I really feel that Jesus the Carpenter has built me a new life: far away from the barrack gate. My remarkable wife has been a key instrument in making this happen. She has turned the vicarage into a home. She has turned the walled garden into a life filled oasis. If only I had her knack for improving things or causing living things to flourish as never before. In every way she has been my coach, anchor and guide. In every way she has been my true and constant friend.

During the Retirement Course we had some free time. So I went to my room, took out my notebook and the words of this poem started to flow from my pen. Once it was finished I read it back and realised that it neatly summarised this point in my journey. I have indeed become fully part of something new. Something very different to what I have known before. I have worked hard to change and adapt in order to be alongside the people that God has given me in this place. It is true that every day brings something new. I have become something new: in order to live among people who knew each other long before I got here. They will continue to do so, after I have gone. After all, priests and loved ones come and go. As do uniforms and clothes. But some things remain constant and true throughout. This small short poem points to those enduring things that stay with us long after most things have left us.

The final full stop is near. I am ending with a poem that was not written when I started to produce this book. The book itself has become part of my journey and it has added to my journey. With its help, I see more clearly how I got here, what is around me and where I might be going: with what remains of the road in front of me. The words of another traveller are rising inside me until I hear them in the silence of my mind. I mean the one who said, *behold I make all things new.*

Something new is definitely afoot. I have no idea what exactly comes next or how I will get there. I never did. But I will take the next step and the next step until all my steps are taken.

Life as a parish priest is rich and varied. This new life is now a familiar life. Strangers have become friends. Journeys and stories combine. Kindness reveals the treasure of ordinary things. A warm welcome brings another soul in from the cold. All Hallows is a church where all souls are welcome and the healing of memories can begin.

I will continue to change and adapt. As we all must. I know that in my case, ghosts, memories and habits will follow me around. From time to time I will find the wit to embrace all that is challenging, wonderful and new. Yet part of what will give me the strength to do so, is the memory of that place, *where the wild poppies grow…*

Through the eye of the storm   Page 84

We have all passed through the eye of the storm in different ways. Oftentimes it is just life messing with our plans and our heads. Generally making it hard to make headway. Storm clouds block our view. Every simple step becomes a difficult task with uncertain results. There is nothing personal about storms like this.

Sometimes though it is personal because the storms we enter against our will are often caused by the ill will of other people. Being on the receiving end is a buffeting unpleasant experience in which our small boat is tossed about by waves of human origin and design. Those radioactive souls can so easily contaminate the souls of those who already question their own worth. The path we seek becomes obscured and the decisions we try to make for good become a perfect storm of confusing signals, messages and actions.

Sadly, it is true, that the negativity of a few or even just one: can take a good day for many and turn it into a bad day for many. One of the biggest challenges for any of us is to turn a negative into a positive. To recycle the storm waters that are no longer fit for human consumption. So the thirsty can drink in safety knowing full well whom they can trust to help them take the next step.

Putting the finishing touches to this book has obliged me to reflect deeply and widely about my sixty-one years on this earth. The subject matter of this poem is not pleasant and is not easily addressed. But we all have to address it if we are not to be undermined by it. So in my own small way: I have looked it in the eye. And to my surprise I ended up with a composite picture of difficult people that I have known over the years. Too often they were the very ones I tried to encourage and support.

In the end, with some of them, I came to see that changing them was something beyond my grasp. No doubt some of them perceived me as difficult. Be that as it may, and come what may, I want to change for the better. I am willing to change for the better. I know that if true friends fail to tell me where I am getting it wrong then I will never improve but always stay the same. But as this poem progressed I also saw my need to sort myself out. To pass through the eye of the storm and emerge back into the light where we all belong.

That means breaking from the power of the storm. Whether that storm is caused by the impersonal forces of nature and daily life or the very personal kind of storms that are created by those we once trusted but for whom we continue to pray. The only way to deal with meddlers is to join those who prefer to be mediators. For me the image of a small boy free to fly his kite is the heavenly glimmer of a brighter light…

Kevin Bell
All Hallows Church
Twickenham
2019

About the Author

Kevin Bell served in *The British Army* for more than twenty-six years. The poems selected for this volume reflect his experience at home and overseas. He witnessed *The Cold War* become a series of hot wars, a divided Germany become a united Germany, and *The Troubles* become *The Good Friday Agreement*. In the UK he dealt personally with the consequences of campaigns in Iraq and Afghanistan. He did so chiefly via those heart-breaking Repatriation Ceremonies.

Through a series of promotions he worked in many countries including Bosnia and Kosovo. His role as a senior chaplain brought joys and challenges in equal measure. Inside that public journey there was a private more personal journey. Writing poetry helped him to find a way through. Doing so meant that he was better placed to help those around him.

Retirement from the army in 2015 caused a return to life as a parish priest. That work includes care of the local RAF Air Cadets. At the national level he also gives some time to the welfare of military veterans.

Photo – Canada on a Live Fire Exercise in 1996 © Kevin Bell

Kevin has written poems since his teens. In many ways they have been an essential part of his life and ministry: a spiritual discipline of sorts that has enabled him to fulfil his public duties. With this volume he is going public in a good cause. This has only been possible with his return to civilian life. For military service did not give the time or stability to attend to such projects.

He is also a songwriter. This too has been a private pastime until now. Returning to parish ministry has allowed him to record a debut album in his off duty moments. Fourteen of his songs appear with him playing six string guitar, twelve string guitar and the harmonica. *Answers for the brave...* is being released alongside this book.

From the Author

"There are many things that can only be seen through eyes that have cried

(Oscar Romero)

Tears of joy and sadness have a curious capacity to improve human sight. I have seen this in others and I have felt it in myself. Through all the separations, reunions and final goodbyes, our vision becomes blurred before it is restored. Quickly or slowly: it returns to us more fully, than before our hearts were moved. Those who are with us: can speed or slow the process. A broken heart can heal like a broken wing and a breaking voice can learn once more, to laugh and sing. These are the wonders of the human soul: through joy, through sadness, and through everything in between.

The poems chosen for this little book, all speak to the theme of remembering and remembrance. In different ways they met my need: *to see more clearly, follow more nearly and love more dearly*, as St Richard of Chichester implored us to do. But the words that came to my heart and pen, were also my pastoral response to those I met or was travelling with. I now realise that my private scribbles are also something more. *Native Americans* have a wise and insightful saying about human beings: *we all leave tracks...* Indeed, we miss the point if we think that only animals leave tracks. These poems are just some of the tracks that I have left behind me, as I continue to go forward, as we all must do, by one means or another: *through the joy, through tears, and through everything in between.*

Photo – All Souls Requiem Mass in 2018 © Denise Quinlan

Those who have kindly lifted their pens in support of this book are not responsible for my views or my mode of expression. I am deeply grateful that by supporting me they have also supported a very worthy cause.

Finally, my deepest gratitude goes to my wife and adult children, who supported me through many years of military service, with never a word of complaint. I can never repay what they have given to me, or fully express what they mean to me…

Father Kevin Bell,
MA FRSA

Published Papers

The following three articles

Were

Originally published

In

'The British Army Review'

The Heart and the Heat of Battle

Photo – Bosnia in 1997 © Kevin Bell

On Patrol, Nad-e-Ali, Afghanistan

THE HEART AND HEAT OF BATTLE [43]

Introduction [44]

At the heart of any battle is the human heart. For instance, the hearts that sleep in this cemetery were once like yours and mine. Hopes and fears lived side by side with loves and hates. Generosity and courage lived side by side with meanness and panic. Like those remembered here, we are capable of so many wonderful things. Sadly we are also capable of so many dreadful things. In those life or death moments things can go either way. The heat of battle can be literally hot bullets and shells whizzing through the air in your direction. Perhaps the heat of battle can also refer to the heat and pressure of trying to do the right thing when everything around you, is pushing you, towards the wrong thing. There will even be times when right or wrong just blur into one ugly picture. When you can no longer see the wood for the trees, when that one good thing is unable to stand out from the crowd; at such times, what on earth is a soldier to do?

---

[43] Written by the Reverend Kevin Bell MA CF, when serving as Assistant Chaplain-General, 3rd (United Kingdom) Division 2011.
[44] In June 2011, after several open-air church services, there followed a battlefield tour of the American Landings. At Omaha Beach there is a large US Military Cemetery. Following a talk by a military historian, this address was given by the Divisional Padre:

If there is no clear choice, how will the officer decide what to do next?

The Need for Character

The truth of what I am introducing here is born out very well by a former General of the US Army. He rose through the ranks and served with distinction. In retirement he wrote books on military history. He produced some solid work about the American Civil-War with particular interest in the Confederate Armies. He wrote as an historian but we can still see his own experience of war coming through in what he wrote. As we look on this Cemetery it is worth pausing to hear his words:

> "No one who has ever been under fire during combat, whether on land, or sea, or in the air, will deny that at such times a soldier's true character is revealed. Then it is that the men are separated from the boys, in a positive way that cannot be misunderstood by their fellow soldiers. There is no time to dissemble or play a part; death may strike at any moment, and under such tense conditions a man's soul is bared and his true character nakedly revealed by what he says and does or does not do." [45]

These words carry the authority of a man who had been to war several times. He knew what he was talking about. To put it bluntly, the character and content of the human heart will guide you when there is little left to show you the way. If character and content are poor then the human heart will let you down: it simply will not be fit for purpose, it will not be equal to the awful task. Of course training and conditioning have a role to play. But in the heat of battle, the head must decide what to do with that training and conditioning. The heart must find courage to act or even, to hold back. Character will make the difference.

The Impact of Rank

Is it the same for everybody regardless of rank? Again the same author comes to our aid. This is what he wrote:

> "The principal difference between the man in the ranks and the General of the army at such times is the extent to which the individual's attitude and actions influence and have impact on the lives and fortunes of others. The cowardly soldier who dares not face death, but chooses to drop into a convenient shell hole while his companions go forward in the face of enemy fire, may

---

[45] Page 170 – *Chancellorsville: 2nd Edition* – By General Edward Stackpole. Stackpole Books; 1988, USA

or may not influence the course of the battle. But the captain, or colonel, or general, who is deficient in moral and physical courage, bears the awful responsibility of the lives of hundreds of thousands of his fellowmen who depend on him and are sworn to obey his orders." [46]

It is hard to comment on strong opinions born from long experience of war. I would simply add this: whatever rank we are privileged to carry, we all carry the honour of wearing the Queen's uniform. We do it in good times or in bad. We may be judged by how smartly we wear it. We will certainly be judged by how well we carry it. Do we add to its honour and prestige or do we make it harder for others to see our uniform as a force for good in this troubled world.

Living with choices
Old soldiers look back over their pint of beer or their glass of wine and reflect about the uniform they once wore with pride. General Sir David Fraser looked back on his time as a young officer fighting in France during the Second World War. As the Normandy Campaign unfolded many German Prisoners of War were taken and the imagery lived with him as an old man. But one image in particular continued to trouble him.

> "I can, however, see one picture which I greatly regret, and which was probably not unique. A few enemy soldiers, perhaps four, were lined up on a small plot of grass beside a minor road, parallel to the one on which I was travelling. They seemed to be under guard of perhaps two of our own men, who were obviously making them turn out their pockets, hand over desirables like watches. This, of course, was wholly illegal but it happened.
>
> A few minutes later I happened to turn my binoculars back on this parallel road, by now some distance away. I saw what looked like four huddles of field grey, now on the ground, inert." [47]

With remarkable honesty this Guards Officer goes on to discuss his own reactions to what he had witnessed all those years ago.

> "I was on some mission or other. I did not immediately drive across, find the place, investigate. Sometimes a man of ours

---

[46] Page 170 – *Chancellorsville: 2nd Edition* – General Edward J Stackpole: Stackpole Books; 1988, USA
[47] Page 226 – *Wars and Shadows: Memoirs of General Sir David Fraser* – David Fraser: Penguin Books: London, 2002

would (it was muttered) become 'trigger happy'. Sometimes he had, perhaps, lost a particular friend and hatred possessed him so that he turned on the defenceless. None of this is excusable and nor is my own non-investigation. For our record had blemishes and some of them were, by repute, ugly. One heard (not in our own Grenadier Group) of claims – boasts almost – that 'we didn't intend to take any prisoners', during a particular battle or phase of the campaign. Such brutality was not necessarily described accurately; some people feel more robust for the ability not to flinch from cruel conduct and brag accordingly; but there was here and there an under-current of inhumanity and it jarred. It jars still. I had looked the other way." [48]

Burned deep in the memory of this brave old man is a warning for all of us in uniform. I mean that the danger of looking the other way, is a two edged sword. Yes it will cut you at the time. War may rob you of your youth. *Looking away* may rob you of a good night's sleep. You may hope to get older and wiser with the passing of years. But the second cut may prove the deepest and the hardest to heal. It may reduce your sense of being human. It may add to your struggle to be humane. As that British officer found to his cost, looking away caused regret. I think he was hard on himself. After all, he was only twenty-three. But I cannot deny him, his own assessment of himself, as he thought back to those German POWs, executed by soldiers who wore the same uniform as him. For me those final words of his have a haunting quality:

"…there was here and there an under-current of inhumanity and it jarred. It jars still.
I had looked the other way." [49]

The example given shows the importance of paying attention instead of looking away. We may walk away with a clean conscious and our reputation intact. On the other hand, we may spend a lifetime living with choices made in the heat of the moment or the cold light of day.

Assessing the Enemy
How a soldier of conscience views his enemy is equally important for us to consider. In this case, he saw a difference between SS and Gestapo Units in the Concentration Camps or accused of war crimes against civilians. In

---

[48] Page 226 – *Wars and Shadows: Memoirs of General Sir David Fraser* – David Fraser: Penguin Books: London, 2002
[49] IBID

those instances he said. "The SS were named as perpetrators and this seemed to justify counter-brutality without restraint." [50]

It is perhaps surprising then to hear his thoughts on this difficult matter:

> "...The Waffen SS, against whom we fought, were a completely separate part of the organization from the concentration camp guards, the Gestapo and the like. They were very well-disciplined, well-trained, well-led and outstanding soldiers; and they deserved to be treated as such by their enemies except in particular and rare cases." [51]

He then goes on to quote from a letter home that he wrote on 16th September 1944:

> "The SS are magnificent, a great thorn in our sides. We captured an SS officer the other day who talked long and seriously. `1940 was our hour`. he said, `and there's no doubt 1944 is yours`. He gave it two months to total collapse but he was completely confident that in a few years they'd be back. He said they'd had to shoot a lot of Poles, Russians, French, etc because of the `Terrorism` and perpetual attacks on German soldiers and supply columns and sabotage - `when fighting for one's life one cannot tolerate such things - surely you as a soldier understand that?' He was indignant about the bombing - `You began it. Cologne was the first city bombed.' He'd fought three campaigns in Russia: North Africa: Tunisia, Italy, France (1940) and France (1944). He'd been wounded five times (severely) and had a Typhoon splinter in the chest at the time of capture. But all he wanted was another go." [52]

That was his letter home. Many years later as an old man he reflected on what he had written as young man.

> "I wrote as a no doubt naïve twenty-three year old, but such men merited the honour due to warriors, if anybody did. And most of our opponents were not, in any case, SS." [53]

---

[50] IBID
[51] Pages 226-227 - *Wars and Shadows: Memoirs of General Sir David Fraser* – David Fraser: Penguin Books: London, 2002
[52] Page 227 – IBID
[53] IBID

A Health Warning
General Fraser and his like were remarkable soldiers and brave men. He was clearly a moral man with an ethical code by which he tried to operate. However, it seems he made a big mistake in assessing his enemy. We must not make the same mistake. A military assessment is not the same as a moral or ethical assessment. The SS may have been *"well-disciplined, well-trained, well-led and outstanding soldiers..."*

They may have been brave and determined. But no body would say they were ethical, moral, right or deserving of respect. I respectfully suggest he has the right to admire the fighting qualities of those he met in battle. Yet I believe it is unhealthy to make any moral claim for the SS or distinguish them from SS Guards in Concentration Camps. All the SS championed a bad cause that led to war crimes and court cases. Their fighting efficiency does not make them good men in a bad cause...

Rather it means their skill in combat prolonged the reign of Nazi terror over the lives of millions. By implication, not just the SS but the entire German war machine aided and abetted the SS in their ethical code and conduct. We can allow that outside the SS there were Germans in uniform who questioned the Nazi cause.

However, most of them fought so strongly that it took the world to stop them. Indeed, very few were part of the plot to remove Adolf Hitler. The vast majority soldiered on. Their conduct in battle is all we can judge them by. Their treatment of the civilian population in many recorded cases makes it very difficult for us to take seriously any individual doubts that may have existence.

After the war in the Nuremburg-Trials, some defendants pleaded that they had no choice, that they were merely *"Following Orders"*. That plea was dismissed by *International Law* and the *Free World*. It remains a powerful principle for all in uniform that we must be men and women of conscience who do not blindly follow Orders. We must have heart, character and a robust ethical code. We must remain human and act humanely. We too will be judged by our actions rather than our words. Law courts and history will look to our actions and conduct, as the only visible clue to the contents of our hearts and character. We will be judged with the same measure by which we judge our enemy. We must be healthy and wholesome in every way. It is better to shine than to smell.

Assessing our Own Times

The uniform we wear is rather different to the one worn by General Fraser. It is still British but it is worn in a very different world to the one he knew. Since World War Two, many of our enemies have been in uniforms of one kind or another. But in recent years most of our enemies have not worn any kind of recognizable uniform. Their tactics are those of the guerrilla-fighter or the terrorist. In truth, we do our best and proudly wear our uniforms. They on the other hand, do their worst, only to melt back into the crowd where genuine civilians fear to look them in the eye.

It is hard for us to put our enemies on a scale of one-to-ten in order to measure their badness or seeming lack of morals, as we judge and understand them. Soldiers of the *Wehrmacht* are judged more moral than those of the *SS*. We differentiate between ordinary members of Saddam Hussein's Army and Units of *The Republican Guard*. The *Mujahedeen-fighters* were clearly different from the *Taleban*. The IRA and their modern variants act similarly but are motivated very differently when compared with *al-Qaida*.

Civilian Conduct in War

For our soldiers, sorting the good guys from the bad guys; is much more difficult than in days gone by. How can we operate a scale of one-to-ten in any meaningful way? Should we apply the same scale to ourselves? Certainly! Can we apply a similar scale when assessing the conduct of civilian populations around the world? General Fraser was brave enough to try to do so. It is clear from what he wrote that this proved a difficult and uncomfortable task born from disturbing experiences in wartime France. He felt particular disgust at the treatment of female collaborators. Fraser was human enough to allow that these women had acted from a variety of reasons: greed, fear, desire, genuine human feelings and in some cases, even for reasons of love. [54]

Nonetheless, he paints a grim picture of civilian ethics in time of war.

> "It was, therefore, frequent to enter a place from which the Germans had recently withdrawn and to find one or two pitiful, whimpering women, clothes half torn from their backs, hair roughly and totally shaved so that they were disfigured and shamed, often bearing marks of beating and ill-treatment, surrounded by jeering groups of Frenchmen and Frenchwomen…

---

[54] Page 224 - *Wars and Shadows: Memoirs of General Sir David Fraser* – David Fraser: Penguin Books: London, 2002

We had not suffered as these bullies had probably suffered. We had not lived under German occupation. It did not lie with us to suppress this cruelty. It was not for us to pass judgement, so we drove on, through cheering crowds.... I remember one particular place, a small town or village, where the gutter in the long main street was actually running with blood, although there had been no battle there. The blood was the blood of French girls, some of whom were crouched pathetically on doorsteps, hiding their faces and their shame, beaten up, pouring out their grief..." [55]

In Bosnia, Kosovo and more recent campaigns, British soldiers have continued to learn these difficult lessons. We may liberate from tyranny or genocide, we may fan the flames of freedom and democracy, only to witness, hatred and revenge played out before our eyes, in all their ugly detail. At such times, we may be left wondering about the meaning of our own sacrifices and if those we came to help, truly value the blood we spilt or the sacrifices that we made, for their sake. Perhaps at those times, the hardest part of being a soldier, is finding a way to live with yourself when those you are trying to help, seem incapable of living with themselves or their neighbours.

The After-Shocks of War
Such things are difficult to bear if you are journalist looking on, or an *NGO* (Non Government Organization) charity worker desperately trying to help. I think such things are especially hard for those in uniform who risked their lives to make things better. I suggest that these things are close to the heart and the heat of what it means to be a soldier. The war itself may be seen and felt as a kind of *Earthquake*. These reprisals may be seen as the *Aftershock* directly related to the original event. For the soldier the *Earthquake* and the *Aftershock* are seen and felt just as deeply. This is so because the soldier fought a deadly determined foe that ordinary people might live without fear. Once those people have been liberated they can finally choose just how human they really want to be. In South Africa for instance, they opted for peace and reconciliation without revenge. It was a deeply painful experience for former victims of oppression, or those who felt they had been betrayed by collaborators: to see the guilty walk free must have been hard to bear, even if it was for the greater good and the hope of a better South Africa.

Sadly history teaches us that such examples are rare. Instead, we have a creed that says, *"Don't get mad, get even."*

---

[55] Page 225 – IBID

In wartime France a few lived by that creed once their country had been freed. I wonder if their *Getting Even* brought any lasting peace to their hearts or cooled the heat of their hurts? Others, perhaps most, found all their energies consumed by picking up the pieces and trying to move on: they did not have the time or the energy, for hatred or revenge; they just wanted to be human again and rebuild their shattered lives.

An Ethical Line in the Sand

For soldiers still fighting in other parts of France, their moral choices were far from black-and-white. General Fraser gives the classic example that could be applied to any war. It demonstrates that the ethical line in war may not be set in concrete but written in sand.

> "A British platoon might be fired upon by a German post and finally storm it. Fire – German fire – might be kept up against attackers (bravely and effectively, causing casualties) until the last moment, and then the defenders would emerge, hands on high...
> In such circumstances it is rare that quarter will be given. Blood is up, and if it were not men would not assault. Comrades have fallen. Surrender could have been earlier. The rest is imaginable..." [56]

I am not a fighting man but I am proud to be a military man. As a Christian priest in military service, I accept that such events are part of the grim realities of war.

I believe that the *Profession of Arms* is an, honourable one. This is especially true when it is sometimes necessary to employ the *Lawful-use of Lethal-force*. This must always be done as a last resort, with sadness and regret, but with firm resolve. Sometimes it is necessary to take life in order to save life. Indeed, were it not for D-Day, and similar costly events, there would be few if any Jews on this planet and much of the free world would be enslaved. Historians will judge if our cause was just and how well we fought. Winning the peace will be helped or hindered by how humanely we managed to win the war. Did we observe the line set in concrete? Did we try hard to draw that line in the sand?

Winning the Peace

---

[56] Page 227 - *Wars and Shadows: Memoirs of General Sir David Fraser* – David Fraser: Penguin Books: London, 2002

When armies get it wrong then the smell of atrocities may overpower even the sweetest garlands of peace. What happens though when the war is over and some kind of peace has been won?

Well that is the time when every body must live with the decisions they made and the things they did. They may even have to learn to live with the things they failed to do. How might the British public for instance respond to our dead or wounded soldiers? For over four years now I have taken my turn at Repatriation Ceremonies in the UK. We have all been moved by public displays of affection, gratitude and mourning. The market town of Wooten-Bassett is a prime example of what I mean. In 2010 I went to Winchester Cathedral for the Memorial Service held in honour of *11 Light Brigade* upon their return from Afghanistan. Royalty, VIPs and all sorts piled into that historic Christian building. Last of all two mini-buses pulled up and let out wounded soldiers in desert uniforms. Several had lost limbs. Some bore other scars of battle. I suspect all had inner scars that also need healing. However, as they hobbled forward on crutches or in wheelchairs, the cheers and applause of the crowds, grew louder and louder. In fact, the greeting for those soldiers was the most audible and most moving of the day. The net result was that every body felt ten feet tall and heart felt pride was the order of the day.

Perhaps that image is the one to remember whenever we are tempted to do wrong in war. I mean it would be awful if our decisions and actions diminished in any way, the respect shown to those wounded soldiers. The *Cleanness* of our military history must stand up to scrutiny when the history books are written about events in which our comrades serve.

How Best to Remember
As we think of our comrades who have fallen, or the brave young men remembered in this War-Cemetery, let me take you back to the First World War. By doing so, I aim to give an example of the way in which I would like every fallen or wounded British soldier to be remember. "Writing in early 1917, Eva Isaacs tells her husband of a dinner party where one of the guests was Cecil Langton, an officer blinded in the war:

> "Poor Chap, it makes one's heart ache to see him. I feel as if I was his debtor for life, for after all it was for me and all of us at home that he lost his sight. I feel much the same to all the wounded I see or for that matter anyone in Khaki. They seem to have a tremendous hold on one, nothing one can do is enough

and one can never repay them for all they have lost or all they have risked." [57]

For the sake of all our wounded and fallen, and for all the reasons I have given above, we must take care how we live our lives in peace and war. We wear the Queen's uniform and will rightly be judged more harshly than any civilian. As the Bible reminds us, *"much is expected of him to whom much has been given."* [58]

However, I am very aware that we are in France. I have read that Napoleon valued two things above all others in military commanders. First he valued *"high moral courage, capable of great resolution."* Only second came, *"Physical courage, which takes no account of danger."* [59]

Conclusion
Finally, it seems logical to suggest that if Napoleon wanted this for his commanders then he also wanted this for all his soldiers. We should want this for British soldiers, especially those who serve in *The 3rd Division*: *"High moral courage, capable or great resolution"* and *"Physical courage, which takes no account of danger."* With these qualities we can endure the heart and heat of battle!

Let us pray
May the God whom we serve, welcome our fallen comrades, and heal their wounds, in readiness for eternal life. May he strengthen our bereaved and wounded! As they seek to carry on. May he guide and reassure us in all our decisions and actions. That when our battles are over. We may enjoy a lasting peace, in which our regrets if any are kept to a minimum. We ask these things in the name of Jesus Christ our Lord. That with him, the souls of the faithful departed: may rest in peace and rise in glory. Amen.

End

---

[57] Page 112 – *The Last Great War: British Society and the First World War* – By Adrian Gregory. Cambridge University Press, 2008
[58] Bible – Luke 12.48
[59] Page 368 - *Chancellorsville: 2nd Edition* – General Edward J Stackpole: Stackpole Books; 1988, USA

Remembrance Sunday

Photo – Remembrance Sunday 2018 © Jan Collins

A Quick Turn Around, Maysaan, Iraq

REMEMBRANCE SUNDAY [60]

Why the silence?

At *Bergen-Belsen* you will find stillness and silence. It is there on a crowded day like background radiation. Turning up early or late in the day can result in being almost alone. It is then that the stillness and the silence can become unbearable. Many years ago I lasted just twenty minutes on my own. After that I had to escape via the nearest exit.

Most adults have felt a similar need to escape especially when an awkward silence destroys the happy atmosphere in a crowded room.

Torture through sensory deprivation is achieved via solitary confinement. A key part of that can be speakers producing white noise. Yet it can also be the enforcement of silence and stillness. Basically, depriving one human being of the noise and movement of another human being.

How curious then that stillness and silence are the core ingredients of Remembrance Sunday?

---

[60] I wrote this whilst serving as Senior Chaplain to the Household Division where I was based at the Guards' Chapel in London. A version of this article was published in the *British Army Review* in the autumn of 2013: Edition Number 158

Indeed, for two whole minutes we stand in stillness and silence. Some will sit in a wheel chair and add to the weight of the silence: their stillness increasing the awkwardness we try to suppress because we are still intact and scar free.

Moreover we pause to remember fallen comrades, the experience of war and our cherishing of peace in a free and democratic land.

Alongside these observations about silence I reflect on more than twenty-five years as an army chaplain. Like me you may recall those first lessons in *Combat First Aid*. We were told that in assessing the wounded we should not rush to the ones who scream or make lots of noise. Rather we should seek out the ones who are very quiet. This is because they are very often the most badly injured.

Unlike me, you have probably not been ordained since 1983. Through all those years of funerals, bereavement and sadness, I have learned a similar lesson. Namely, in the funeral or afterwards at the wake, it is not always obvious that the noisy tearful moving people are the ones hurting most deeply. Very often I have found that it is those who are still and silent who are actually hurting the deepest and grieving the most. As a Church of England priest I do my best to minister to all. However, turning up at the wake and seeking out the quiet soul in the corner has often opened up to me a special heart and allowed me to help. They tend to be the ones who leave early.

In the same way that for most of us, two minutes silence, is plenty and the second trumpet blast is a welcome return to normality. To put it another way: *"Mankind cannot bear very much reality"*. [61]

If I am right about all of this then wrapping uniforms, medals, hymns, prayers, parades, prayers and poppies, around Remembrance Sunday is one sure way to limit our exposure to too much reality: too much stillness and silence. Yet like the man or woman at the wake, those two minutes, that central act of remembrance, is the main place where we remember the cost of war, the price of peace, the pain of bereavement and the joy of healing.

---

[61] I believe this comes from the author Somerset Maugham or the poet, TS Elliot

Approaches
I have preached Remembrance Sunday in many places. In recent years, one place in particular stays in my mind. On Salisbury Plain you will find St George's Memorial Church in Bulford. Much of it was built with money given by soldiers returning from the Great War. They wanted to say *"Thank you"* for coming home to the girl they loved. But they also wanted to remember their mates who did not make it. That church belongs to the present generation of soldiers. It was made possible by soldiers like them from an earlier generation.

Today you will find huge brass memorial plaques to those we have lost in Iraq and Afghanistan. Already those large proud shinning names have almost filled the spaces that were originally provided. In that church, for three years in a row, I saw people wearing the distinctive *Elizabeth Cross*. I think it is brilliant that our Sovereign chooses to acknowledge the loss of loved ones in such a unique way. Year by year we remember soldiers, sailors and airmen who fought in two world wars. We also remember more recent conflicts. We salute the courage, professionalism and sacrifice of our fallen comrades. We pray for the bereaved and the wounded.

Throughout this island home, a grateful nation stands with us in proud silence to remember these things and to give thanks for all who guard our liberties by wearing the uniform of Her Majesty the Queen. But these days, wherever Remembrance Sunday is commemorated, it is clear that we have all been touched in some way by the death or wounding of a comrade. We each have reasons to remember. It is my job as a chaplain, to speak to the feelings and memories that fill human hearts in churches, hangars, parade squares, schools, shops and all manner of public places.

Aspects
Those who have never read the bible may well have read words from it without realizing. *"Greater love has no man than to lay down his life for his friends."* These words from the lips of Jesus are perhaps the ones most often seen on war memorials. I think those particular words speak well of our soldiers, sailors and airmen. They do lay down their lives for their friends. But I have come to believe that they go further than this. Indeed they have been known to lay down their lives for complete strangers. I know of one case where a British officer won the Military Cross going to the aid of an officer in the Afghan Army. Such an act of heroism has huge cultural and religious significance. I hope such stories will become better known when the war is over. To risk your life for friend and stranger is more than most people are prepared to even consider. But it is clear to me that British soldiers have even risked **all** for their **enemy.**

This famously happened in Northern Ireland at a police station. An explosive device of some description had been thrown into the station and there were innocent people inside. There was not enough time to safely get it away, so the soldier threw himself on top of it. He saved the lives of those nearby including women and children. But outside people jeered when they learned that a British soldier had been killed. He received a Posthumous George Cross.[62]

Similar things have happened in Iraq and Afghanistan. Some of our own have risked all to make the world a better place. It used to be that women teachers were beheaded in front of their class. Or a hand grenade was thrown into a classroom full of little girls. People in uniforms like ours have died in order to stop such things happening. Our brave selfless comrades have laid down their lives for a better Iraq and a better Afghanistan. One day, please God, our enemies will realize the difference we made. They may also realize how illiteracy, ignorance, hatred and fear, were driven back, in hope of a better world, for friends, strangers and enemies.

Questions
For me, Remembrance Sunday comes down to two basic questions. *"How best to Remember"* and *"How best to carry on."* There is one mental image that helps me when trying to hold it all together in my head. Consider: a vast parade ground between us and them and if we look hard, we can see that they are returning our salute. They cheer us on. Moreover, they are waiting for us, and the time when Old Comrades will be reunited.

As a Christian priest I believe in life after death just as much as I believe in life before death. Experience has taught me that the veil between this life and the next is often very thin. Only a whisper separates us. A prayer can be heard either side of the great divide: as the Church on earth is united with the Church in heaven: I believe that soldiers on earth are somehow united with their fallen comrades on the other side. We have not stopped loving them or praying for them. They still love us and wish us well with all that we still have to do, until we can see them again. Our task is not to let them down but to remember well, and to carry on, as best we can.

---

[62] Lt Gen John Lorimer DSO MBE (Late Para) was my GOC at 3 DIV when I used this illustration in a sermon. He afterwards confirmed the details via an email.

History

The challenges of war have been dramatically relearned by a new generation of British soldiers. I am no military historian but in World War One, I believe the average death toll was around 15,000 per week. In World War Two, the average number of deaths per week was around 5,000. Thank God we do not have to deal with such staggering statistics. Our own numbers in recent years have been significant. I am no statistician. But proportional to the size of the Force, our losses have been the same as our American Allies. Not in terms of actual numbers. Rather, in terms of the emotional and psychological effects on that Force. The pain is proportionate and there is no denying that we have absorbed our full share.

With these thoughts in mind, I remember talking to an old bishop who confirmed me when I was a young civilian policeman. He has been an Army Padre in World War Two taking part in the D-Day Landings. He earned the Military Cross rescuing the wounded from behind enemy lines and under fire. I told him I felt such a wimp because our losses seemed so small compared to his and yet they affect us all so badly. He said something amazing. *"We felt every one just the* same *but we had to carry on."* His reply stunned me and left me with even more respect and admiration for his remarkable, uncomplaining generation. Like them, we have to carry on.

Another fine example of that generation is the Normandy Veterans. I was serving as Divisional Padre with the 3rd Division. They led the annual D-Day Commemorations in Normandy. Some of us were privileged to go over each year. We did about eight parades and open air Services in just three days. I was tired afterwards, until I realized that those old boys had been to every one and in the bar most nights. No wonder they won in the end. There was always a fine military band. In each location local dignitaries and ordinary people turned out to welcome the Veterans and provide some generous 'hospitality'.

On one occasion I was talking with a deputy mayor who was also a farmer. I asked him straight. *"What do these old men really mean to you?"* His reply was deeply moving. *"Every day I thank God for these old men. Because of them I can speak my language, and I can plough my fields. That is what they mean to me."*

On different occasion, a member of the French Resistance took off the little blue lapel badge he was wearing and gave it to me. Apparently, it is the cornflower and the symbol of France. He did not speak English but a local woman translated what he said. "He wants you to have this. He says he wants to say *"Thank you" to you for your soldiers, and for the freedom of France."* I now wear it every Remembrance Sunday. I am probably incorrectly dressed when wearing it anywhere near our own red poppy. But I am going to keep it anyway, in memory of our Normandy Veterans.

Another memory from those Normandy visits came on my last trip. We were at a wonderful reception with the local mayor and townspeople. The locals had been entertaining us with traditional songs. Suddenly three old veterans, with loads of medals, got to their feet and seized the microphone. Then they led us all in singing the title song from the TV Series Dad's Army. The French people looked on bemused but we all knew the words and joined in. I can still hear them singing those cheeky words. Suddenly they were young men again, teasing about stopping Hitler in his tracks. God bless them: *they did.*

Today
History will show that the same humanity and fighting spirit, is very much alive in the modern British Soldier. In recent years we have suffered slow but steady losses in Iraq and Afghanistan. For many of us this has been like the steady drip-drip-drip of *Chinese-Water-Torture.*

Repatriations
Since 2007 I have taken my turn with Repatriations in the United Kingdom. In the years since, I have met and prayed with many grieving families. Following that we all go outside and take our places. My place is at the back of the huge aircraft. There I wait for yet another soldier to be carried shoulder height in triumph and sorrow. The Union Jack is draped on top in the all too familiar scene. Slowly, comrades from the same regiment ease him out of the aircraft and back onto British soil. The bugle cracks the air or a lone piper weeps on the wind. At that point, I whisper very quiet prayers, to welcome him home and to see him on his final journey. I am not going to share all those prayers. I believe they are between God, the soldier and me. Maybe when I have retired. But I will share these few lines:

> *"I pray, the wounds that could not be healed on earth:*
> *Will be healed in heaven.*
>
> *I also pray, that young lives cut short in this life*
> *Will know Eternity and length of days*

> *In the new life,*
> *I trust they have already begun."*

After one of these ceremonies I read what the Commanding Officer had written about his fallen soldier. Out of respect for the family and others, I will not give details but preserve some anonymity. However, I will quote a small part of what that officer wrote:

> *"Stand Easy Comrade, your duty is done. Your sacrifice will not be in vain*
> *And our success will be your legacy. We will never forget you."*

Soaking up pride and pain in equal measure has not been easy for any of us. But I am under no illusions about my own small part. After each ceremony I can go home and try to sleep it off. Yet I know that those families must carry that burden of love for the rest of their lives. I must pay tribute to the RAF for the dignity they have consistently brought to those occasions and the splendid manner in which those ceremonies have been conducted. No easy task in the cold light of day away from the heat and urgency of battle. We in the army have been well served by our comrades in *Sky Blue*.

I also want to commend what is sometimes referred to as *The Buddy System*. Watching out for each other is very important. I was once 'ambushed' in the bar by a very senior Warrant Officer. He pushed to learn how many Repatriations I had been involved. Eventually his concerned persistence won through. I told him how many coffins I had prayed over at that time. He then offered me a drink and an evening to talk it through. God bless him. I thanked him but said that I was *'fine'* and had my own way of dealing with it. I made my way home, had a drink and went to bed early. He had stirred up deep feelings inside me about the whole business. I reached for my bedside notebook and wrote the following poem before falling asleep:

> **RAF Lyneham**
> *I have prayed over the coffins of forty-five soldiers*
> *I have carried the safety of thousands in my prayers*
> *I have winced in my heart at our wounded*
> *I have wept at the loss of our dead*
> *I have stood in the rain on parade*
> *I have wished no more planes here to land*
> *I have looked in the eyes of their loved ones*

I have sat with their silence and pain
I have saluted the pride of their comrades
I have watched bugle and pipe still the wind
I have marvelled the deeds of the young
I have asked that heaven will take them
I have hoped what this earth cannot yield
I have vowed to continue my duties
I have sought for strength to aid theirs
I have remembered these all once were children
I have given thanks for the day they were born
I have known so many just like them
I have been amazed what they take for the norm
I have sensed the peace of the fallen
I have felt their breath on my face
I have been just a drop in the bucket
I have slept as if grief disappears
I have only been part of their journey
I have been honoured that they're part of mine
I have seen medals and banners and flowers
I have watched it played out on a screen
I have wondered at other men's nightmares
I have met veterans of life and its wars
I have discerned in each Repatriation
That nothing I know sounds the same
Save the silent flag of this nation
Where the names of our heroes remain [63]

Sadly, since writing this poem, my tally of fallen soldiers has risen to fifty-two.

I have not done a *Repatriation Ceremony* since September 2012. It appears I am no longer on the list. If so then may be it is for the best. I retire in 2015 and new challenges await me. Yet like others, I would never refuse such an honour. I have always been humbled by the dignity, love and courage of those families and comrades. I know my fellow chaplains will continue to support them all until the last soldier comes home.

Peace
Like the Commanding Officer mentioned earlier, we promise the fallen that we will never forget them. We do this throughout the year but

---

[63] This poem was written in 2011. It was later included in a book: *Slipknot: Selected Poems*: Fast Print Publishing 2012, UK.

especially around the season of Armistice Day and Remembrance Sunday. Looking back over thirty years of ordained life, I too remember our fallen comrades.

I also remember my years as an Anglican parish priest in Birmingham during the 1980s. I was a part-time Hospice Chaplain. In the chapel they had a large cross on the wall. There was a figure of Christ on it. You would expect him to be in fine robes, Risen from the dead, wearing the crown which shows that he is indeed King of kings, Lord of lords, and has conquered death itself. Instead I was met with Christ in simple flowing robes. You could see the crown of thorns around his head, and those terrible wounds in his hands, feet and side. It showed when Jesus rose from the dead, and appeared to his disciples, looking just like that. You may remember his invitation to remember what had happened to him when he was crucified. *"See my wound, touch them and believe."*

For me this image points to something very powerful in human experience. Some wounds are so deep and painful that they never properly heal. What does change is that wounds heal and become scars. Think about it, if the open wound is washed properly and cleaned, it will not get infected later on and become an even bigger mess. If those hidden wounds of the mind, heart and soul, are washed with tears, then they too, will heal properly. But we may be left with scars once those wounds have healed.

The big transformation and proof of healing, is pointed out for us, in that image of the wounded Christ. He had risen from the dead and was healed. Now he could talk about what happened to him without getting all bitter and twisted. He could even tolerate people touching those scars, without them hurting any more. Some of our experiences and those of our comrades; are a bit like that. There comes a time when we can talk about what happened, without getting too upset. At that stage of recovery, we can touch painful memories without them hurting too much. But we have to look after those scars. It would be unwise to expose them to sun bathing for too long. And be prepared that they might itch from time to time.

Yes, my time as a hospice Chaplain taught me that the wounds of Christ and the wounds of men, have a lot in common. To my joy and amazement, every patient in that hospice lived with the wounds of their own illness, and found peace in the end. Christ could have complained. *"Look what they did to me. Look what happened to me. Where were you when I needed you most?"* Instead he bore no grudges and did not feel sorry for himself. Rather, he made them a promise: *"My peace I give to you."*

For me, as an army chaplain, this boils down to one hopeful message: soldiers, who have suffered and endured the horrors of war, can find healing and move on, to know the comfort of peace. This is why I believe the life and message of Christ is still relevant and important, for the wellbeing of modern soldiers.

Prophecy
The job of a prophet is not just to speak about the future. Neither is it just to be wise about the past. Both are important and should not be over played. However, it is perhaps most useful when a prophet interprets and speaks bravely about the present. Believe it or not, being a prophet is part of the vows I took at ordination. The joke about the tortoise is true: it is dangerous for him to stick his neck out but if he does not risk his neck then he will never make any progress in the right direction.

Sometimes as a Padre I must do the same for a greater good. This time I do it as a kind of health warning. You see there is a phrase that I hear too often, in recent years. I think it has come into fashion with some army types because of the wars we have been fighting. I understand what it is behind it: the phrase is well known to all who have serve in the military, it's those two words, *"Man Up."*

Now: in battle or in realistic war training: *"Man up"* is exactly the right attitude. We all know the old saying. *"Train hard: war easy"*. Although it seems to me, as a Christian priest in military service, that there is nothing 'easy' about war, no matter how hard you train. No: I do not have a problem with the plea to *"Man up"* when it is in the right place and at the right time. But when soldiers and officers come to me with personal and professional problems, I often ask it they have been to anybody else first. Too often they say. *"Yes Padre. But they just told me to Man Up."*

Now I have to say that this is not good enough. It is not putting the soldier first. It is not investing in our people. And when we are not fighting or training for war, it tells me that somebody is too lazy, or not fully equipped, to help with the problems of another human being. Our fallen comrades would be horrified because they died believing in an army that prides *its-self* on looking after, *Its - own*.

More than once, a bewildered member of the medical profession has told me about a phone call from the Chain of Command. The message is very clear. It basically says that anyone admitting mental health problems should be drummed out of the army. I am pleased to say that in most cases, my experience of the Chain of Command on mental health issues has been positive. Yet such encounters prove to me that such unhelpful attitudes are still out there getting in the way of military welfare. It is the stigma of mental health. It is the failure to see the analogy of the *'broken leg'* that needs fixing and healing. To use a rugby analogy, the aim of the medical profession is to get people well again. It is also, when possible and right, to get players back into the game.

The Buddy System, Team Spirit, and Tail-End-Charlie, are all key parts of what makes the army work. Yes, there is a time to *"Man up"*. But there are also times when we need to *"Own up"*. One such time, is Remembrance Sunday. We can and should *"Own up"* to those feelings, and painful memories, because tomorrow will be another day. Our flags may fly proudly at *Full-Mast*. But there is sadly every chance that they will sink to *Half-Mast*, more times than we care to imagine.

Remember
The awful truth of war is that people get dis-membered. It is also true that hearts and minds can be torn apart. Jesus spoke powerfully to these difficult truths…

He said to his disciples. *"This is my body broken for you. This is my blood spilt for you. Do this in remembrance of me and know that I am with you always".* In the Service of Holy Communion these words are always repeated. We acknowledge and feel his power to put back together what has been broken or torn apart.

We lesser men in our own way do the same thing every Remembrance Sunday. Think about it: we lovingly *re-member* in our hearts those whom we love but see no longer. Our hearts and mind come together as one. Each of us in deep and often very personal ways, sense that those we miss are with us always. No wonder the Service of Holy Communion was the parting gift of Jesus to his disciples on the night before he died. No wonder I have felt so honoured and moved to give Holy Communion to British soldiers, for so many years, in so many places. God remembers every one of them even if they should forget me.

Summary
On Remembrance Sunday each year, we pause again to remember our fallen comrades, our wounded and our bereaved. We pray for those who continue to serve in harm's way. I have done my best to consider those two key questions. How best to remember? And. How best to carry on? We do not metaphorically pick scabs for the hell of it. Rather we honour our dead by remembering them as surely as they remember us. Together we reach

out for healing and peace. We ask this blessing for those we will never see again in this life. We also seek this blessing for ourselves. We offer traditional prayers, asking that they will. *"Rest in peace and rise in glory"*. And that. *"Light perpetual will shine upon them."* Until we meet again.

I want to finish by sharing some personal thoughts about the poppy. It has become a potent symbol of all that I have tried to express and so much more. It speaks for what we feel and remember as a proud and grateful nation. It speaks for what we hold privately in our hearts. It has come to summarize how best to remember and how best to carry on. I believe that behind all the wrappings and trimmings of much loved ceremonies; it silently points us, without fuss or ceremony, to the key ingredient of our remembering and our carrying on. I refer to the *SILENCE* that grips us when words are not enough to express all that is in our hearts or why we remember, and will never forget.

Poppies
In 1996 I was serving with the Queen's Royal Lancers. They were having a special service and I wrote a poem with them in mind. They heard it first. It was well received. So I used it that year for Remembrance Sunday. I have only once used it since when an atheist senior officer did not want to read from the bible on Remembrance Sunday. He came to see me feeling a bit awkward about the whole thing. I said I would read from the bible. I offered him that poem to read on the one condition that he did not *'Let On'* who the author was.

The poem is called... *Come Walk With Me.*

It appears in this book on page - 05

End

The British Soldier

Photo – Another UK Repatriation Ceremony © Crown copyright

Downtown Basra, Iraq

THE BRITISH SOLDIER [64]

Introduction

The media has grown used to seeing the British Soldier in all political weathers. They have scored his performance, counted his gains, weighed his losses and sifted his character. Changes of uniform have caught their eye. Advances in equipment have raised questions of cost, safety and suitability. Brave days have brought genuine admiration. Shameful days have brought heartfelt consternation. Whenever he is *"Up Against it"* the pendulum of popular support swings in behind him. In between the wars, he binds his wounds and remembers, as the pendulum swings away, to his sadness and dismay. At those times comrades become his constant consolation. I mean the gloriously alive and the gloriously dead.

I am concerned to shed some light on who and what he is. Rather than what he is often perceived to be. I hope that by coming to his assistance in this way others may better know and love the British Soldier. My word is far from final. My opinion is my own. I cannot claim any special relationship or insight. I can speak from the experience of over twenty-five years as an army chaplain. I want to give something back. I am about to retire through the barrack gate. I must say *"Thank you"* before it is too late. Perhaps the best way to achieve this is to say a little about why I became a military chaplain and why I stayed for so long.

Nudges

Various experiences moved me towards the day I became a Chaplain in the British Army. In 1974 I joined the West Midlands Police. I was only sixteen. In November that year I heard evening thunder but saw no storm. The IRA had bombed Birmingham and my hometown would never feel the same. Looking back I realize that other things were changing. I had put on a uniform just in time to see the last of the war generation beginning to retire from police service. In those days we wore tunics and helmets. In several cases, medal ribbons were clearly visibly. Those who wore them were tight lipped about where they had been and what they knew. One was a Lancaster bomber pilot. Another had survived the Burma Railway. There were younger men with a single purple ribbon for service in Northern Ireland.

---

[64] In 2014 this article was published in the *British Army Review*. Retirement from the army would come the following year. I felt the need to remember and reflect before moving on.

In 1980 I left the police and studied in Salisbury to become a priest. The Falklands War took off. In College strong opinions were rehearsed. Yet the ones who were most critical were the same ones who went to Salisbury Plain to watch the military rehearse and then down to the coast to wave off the Task Force Fleet?

I was ordained in 1983. The next few years brought many encounters with former soldiers of all ages. My main effort was parish ministry but for nearly two years I served one day per week as a hospice chaplain. One encounter more than any other nudged me, towards becoming an army chaplain. My future wife was one of the nurses. I turned up one day in 1988 and some visitors were at the bedside of a new elderly patient. I agreed to visit the other wards and come back when he was alone.
Eventually I returned and asked if I could sit beside him. *"Of course you can Padre: be my guest"*. Only an old soldier would call me that. Yet another nudge from God!

We talked and I felt strangely drawn to him. I asked him about his military life. He had been an RSM in the Great War and was called up as Reservist in the second war, also as an RSM. *"That really annoyed the Regulars."* He said, *"Because we delayed their promotions"*.

I asked him to tell me something that I would not find in books. He explained that in the First War rifles would be turned upside down and driven with their bayonets into the muddy ground. Helmets would then be put on top of the rifle butt to show where the wounded soldier lay. He said you could look out and see different helmets: theirs and ours. When a lull in the fighting happened then stretcher-bearers would go out into *No-man's-land* and bring in the wounded. He paused and the look in his eyes grew distant. Only then did he continue.

He said how one day they got all the lads together ready for a big battle. It was the first day they were going to use a new secret weapon that would win the war. It was a foggy misty day. Suddenly these new weapons rolled out. He said the men were terrified and some were ready to run. *"We had to make the crews get out so the lads could see and understand that they were on our side"*.

Next the battle commenced and the tanks rolled towards the enemy disappearing out of sight in the fog.

> *"Suddenly I could hear a terrible sound. It was a crunching sound and the screaming of men. I realized the tanks were*

crushing the upturned rifles and killing our own wounded. I have never forgotten that sound. Every week of my life since then I have woken from my nightmare to the sound of their screams".

I was reduced to respectful mournful silence. Then he piped up. *"Do you mind if I say something to you Padre?"* I replied, *"No, go a head"*. He continued. *"I think you are very brave."* I was stunned. *"I am sorry."* I said. *"I have to disagree. Why on earth do you think I am brave?"* His reply has stayed with me every since:

"I am an old soldier. I am not afraid to go into battle. I would go in the morning. I have been trained and I know what to do. To me this Cancer Ward is a battlefield. I have not been trained. I don't know how to fight it and I am scarred. You don't have to be here and yet you have come onto this battlefield to be with me. That's why I think you are brave".

We said some final things and I promised to pray for him. When I came back next week his bed was empty. I checked with my wife and she confirmed that his last battle was over. I walked out of the building only to have an encounter with another old soldier. *"Excuse me Padre I am with the Arnhem Veterans Association would you like to be our chaplain or can you, recommend somebody? It's just that our old* Padre *has died."* In that moment I made my decision: *"OK God, I give in."*

Courage
The bravery shown in the Great War and at Arnhem was confirmed in the Falklands. In recent years a new generation have displayed that same courage in Iraq and Afghanistan. Yet all these generations are like that RSM in the hospice. He never described himself as man of courage. He did not consider himself brave. He only counted himself as a soldier who had been well trained and knew what to do. He relied on his comrades and not just on himself. He was there for them just as much as they were there for him. How starkly this contrasts with contestants on the TV series *The Apprentice*. There is rarely any hint of such humility or sense of simply doing ones' job. Instead we see young adults who are largely inexperienced human beings yet see themselves as God's gift to the planet and are amazed that Lord Sugar has coped without them until now.

Compassion
Early in my service I befriended a chaplain who served in the first Gulf War. To my ears his story was an unusual one. He was a key member of the Grave Registration Team. Being so new I asked him what this meant. Basically his role kicked in after the Cease Fire. He wore a butcher's apron and had a team of soldiers working with him. They used a bulldozer to dig ditches and it was their job to respectfully find and bury the enemy dead. He told me how moved his soldiers were when they found personal effects among the bodies of their enemy. He mentioned photographs in particular. He was struck by the respect and humanity that they showed. He said they compiled records marking the graves with *eight figure grid references* and *satellite markers*. Apparently when the harrowing task was over the information was sent via diplomatic means to Iraq. His soldiers found it hard to accept that the Iraqi authorities never recovered those bodies. They found it unacceptable that Saddam Hussein would not bring home the men that had died for him. I asked this chaplain how he responded to such difficult questions from his soldiers: *"I simply told them that that is the difference between their army and ours. We care about our soldiers."*

Commitment
In the army we rightly pride ourselves on being available for service on a 24/7 basis. This commitment in principle can lead to the ultimate sacrifice at any time and in any place. Sadly during my time, the principle has become practice, for hundreds killed, and many more with life changing injuries. The cost to their loved ones, in my view, cannot be weighed.

This commitment has consequences little understood by those outside the military community. It fosters and demands a way of life. I mean the army dictates every aspect of a soldier's life, both on and off duty. This was especially so when I first joined up. Indeed, where you live, who you meet, what you do, who your friends are, were clearly defined. One could live in Germany for years and not learn any of the language because we lived in a big bubble called the army. As St Paul remarked. *"The soldier's only concern is to please his Commanding Officer and he does not get involved in civilian affairs"*.

However with the collapse of the Berlin Wall and the Soviet Military threat, there came, the *'Peace Dividend'*. This translated into Government cutbacks of the Armed Forces on a grand scale. This process was known as *'Options for Change'*. By the end of that cull I detected a change in attitude of those who remained. The Army had moved from being a way of life, and was now closer to the civilian attitude of doing a job and booking off. It was still a *24/7* Commitment but it felt more like 9 to 5. Basically people in uniform felt somewhat betrayed. In many cases, the manner in which the news was broken to individuals made their dismissal a bitter experience.

We have since entered another cull of the army and this latest process is still not fully complete. I believe that lessons have been learned and the news is broken with greater compassion and after-care. Nonetheless, the ferocious close quarter battles that many of our soldiers have fought in Iraq and Afghanistan have been closer to the battles of the Second War than the *tit-for-tat* nastiness of Irish Terrorism. With an amateur eye to history, I expect that those de-mobbed after Waterloo, had reason for resentment and cynicism. It is all the more remarkable then that the British soldier puts up, shuts up and get on with job in hand.

Likewise with the Veteran, who may lose his way and end up sleeping rough, or stockpile some bitterness and regret, to share with his mates down the pub. Yet, remains immensely proud of the uniform that was worn and the medals that were earned. In all this we must not forget the Reservist soldier who has earned medals, bled and died or been wounded. They are closer to civilian life than the Regular soldier and visa versa. Indeed they can act as intermediary and interpreter, in the work place, on a Remembrance Parade, or down the pub. Churchill was right to call the Reservist, *"Twice the Citizen"*.

Character
The soldier may be buoyed up by public support. Indeed few of us are indifferent to the good opinion of others. What actor would go on stage night after night with poor reviews and small audiences? That would take massive maturity and artistic integrity. Yet young men mature quickly in war. They go on night after night. They are too busy to read reviews and there is rarely an audience. The difference being that their performance is no act.

When a veteran actor reads critical or even hostile reviews then feelings of irritation and hurt may privately surface. Friends and fellow professionals may reassure that the best thing to do is to carry on. In the cold light of day the Theatre Critic may wield a skilful pen but most have never been an actor. The same is true of the Food Critic who has never been a Chef. To my mind this is equally true of the journalist or the politician who has never worn a uniform. It is easy to sit in judgment on the character and conduct of the solider.

I call this *white-gloved* or *armchair Ethics*. I mean people with clean hands castigating the soldier for having dirty hands. Seemingly unaware they are only kept clean by the willingness of others to get dirty. Charles M Province is a US Army Veteran and some time ago expressed this truth most powerfully:

> *"It is the Soldier, not the minister Who has given us freedom of religion. It is the Soldier, not the reporter Who has given us freedom of the press. It is the Soldier, not the poet Who has given us freedom of speech. It is the Soldier, not the campus organizer Who has given us freedom to protest. It is the Soldier, not the lawyer Who has given us the right to a fair trial. It is the Soldier, not the politician Who has given us the right to vote. It is the Soldier who salutes the flag, Who serves beneath the flag, And whose coffin is draped by the flag, Who allows the protester to burn the flag."* [65]

Humility

The army has six *Core Values* [66] that are taught from *Basic Training*. These are re-enforced throughout the years of military service. They apply in peace and war. They all imply a seventh Value that ought to be explicitly added: humility. When bravery medals are issued and soldiers interviewed, one is deeply moved by the genuine humility that is regularly shown: *"Any one of my mates would have done just the same"*. Or, *"I was only doing my job"*. Or my favourite, when one recipient of a bravery medal was asked what it meant to him: *"I would hand it in just to get back the lads we lost"*.

So ingrained is this humility and team spirit, that soldiers of all ranks, will often sell themselves short, and struggle to get work on leaving the army. On their CV but especially at interview, they will often say, *"We did this"* or *"We did that"*.

Instead of: *"I did this"* or *"I did that"*.

---

[65] He is the Founder and President of the George S. Patton junior Historical Society. He is the Author of several books about this famous US General

[66] Courage, Discipline, Respect for Others, Integrity, Loyalty and Selfless-Commitment

How true it is that big things can hang on little words. I sometimes think that such values are counter-cultural in the modern world. The army seems a relic and a remnant of a world long disappeared. It is now commonplace to broadcast oneself on Twitter, Facebook and Linked-In, with every mention of *"I"* and little mention of *"We"*.

Nonetheless, the military do not have a monopoly on these values. Indeed the policeman, the hospice nurse, or the child caring for a sick parent often display the Core Values of the British Army, in which they have never served. Yet the serving soldier and the veteran do still in my view have something special to share with society at large and if they will not talk about it, then others should, even people like me.

Finally
Soldiers prefer others to tell their story, even if others get it wrong. Soldiers are more concerned about the stories they share with their comrades. Veterans are just the same in my experience. It is important then for historians, politicians, authors and artists, to get alongside soldiers and just listen, to those stories. I mean the ones that can be overheard.

However, it is what soldiers do not say that can sometimes be heard in the silence, on Remembrance Sunday, in the pub or on the Cancer Ward. Indeed when soldiers and veterans fall silent, like that RSM in the hospice, there is often a story that is not being told. I was lucky enough to have heard his story all those years ago. I have been equally lucky, to have been with soldiers for nearly twenty-six years, listening to their stories and listening to their silence. What I have absorbed led me to write a poem meant for soldiers and veterans alike.

That poem is called... *Parade.*

It appears in this book on page - 37

End [67]

---

[67] The following year I did indeed retire after more than twenty-six years as an army chaplain. My appointment as Vicar at All Hallows Twickenham was wonderful. My first month in the parish was also my last month in the army. For several weeks I belonged to two very differently worlds. Then at midnight on my birthday I ceased to be a military man and reclaimed the man I had always been...

A Mirror for the 20th Century

Back to Base, Basra Airfield, Iraq

Holding On, Afghanistan

I Am Strong – Words from Cpl Sean Reeve's pre-deployment letter to his parents. Sean was killed in action, on the last day of his tour in Afghanistan

The Return, Sangin, Afghanistan

"Do not deprive aliens and orphans of justice nor take a widow's cloak in pledge".

Deuteronomy 24: 17

About the Artist

Arabella Dorman is an award winning war artist and one of Britain's leading portrait painters.

Arabella's war art explores the realities of conflict today, its immediate impacts and long-term consequences. Arabella worked as an officially accredited war artist with British Forces in Iraq (2006) and Afghanistan (2009 - 2014) for over a decade, including a month imbedded in Sangin with the 2nd Battalion the Rifles, during the brutal summer of 2009. In more recent years Arabella has worked with refugees and those effected by war in Palestine, Gaza, Lebanon and Syria, resulting in her installations, *Flight* and *Suspended* (St James Piccadilly, Canterbury cathedral, Leicester cathedral 2017-2019) which seek to highlight the humanitarian crisis of forced displacement across the world today. Winner of the Global Mosaic Award 2019, *Suspended* was also shortlisted for the Arts & Christianity Awards 2019.

Arabella enjoys a prominent reputation as a public speaker and fundraiser. She was listed as one of BBC's Top 100 Women in 2014, and Salt Magazine's 100 Most Inspiring Women in 2015. Her work has been profiled across national and international television, radio and print, including New York Times, BBC, CNN, Aljizeera, Radio 4, BBC World Service, and featured on the front cover of The Times, The Guardian and The Sunday Times Magazine.

I have known Kevin Bell since he joined *The Queen's Royal Lancers* in Germany in 1996. Our paths have crossed frequently since then, and I was honoured to attend his Induction as Vicar at *All Hallows Church Twickenham*. He was a great military chaplain. He was always in the right place at the right time, with the knack of understanding what our soldiers were really thinking. He also, always spoke truth to power – a rare quality. So, we all admired, respected and loved him.

These thoughtful - and sometimes haunting – poems, cover a period of high operational tempo for the British Army. I recommend that you read them, slowly over the weeks ahead. You will quickly realise that Padre Kevin cared deeply about those under his spiritual wing. You will also be reminded that there is a price to pay for all our Padres, who are asked to deal, as their daily bread and butter, with the darkest parts of life and death…

General Sir James Everard

– KCB CBE

Arabella Dorman – Is a War Artist with an international reputation. She went to Iraq and Afghanistan with British Forces. She is also an eminent portrait painter. Arabella has generously allowed her paintings to be used in this book. She has also written the Foreword. Do visit her wonderful website: www.arabelladorman.com

Caroline Wyatt - is a distinguished War Correspondent and Journalist. We met at The Guards' Chapel in London where I was Senior Chaplain. I retired from the army in 2015 and became a Vicar in the Diocese of London. In that role I sent Caroline two of my poems. She responded so warmly that I decided to select more poems with a military flavour. She read all of them and encouraged my plans to produce this book.

Remembering and Remembrance are the obvious themes throughout all that I have written in these pages. But it is also important: to give something back. Hence the small but significant charity that I have elected to support with this book.

Please consider supporting those who have paid a price for the freedoms we enjoy.

Kevin Bell *– Vicar of All Hallows Church Twickenham*

A Donation from each book sale will be made to this Charity:

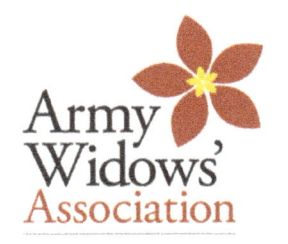

Army Widows' Association

Army Widows Association
Note & Keep
Their Webpage

website@army@armywidows.org.uk